INTERNET USERS' REFERENCE

2002 Edition

TERENA & Netskills

Addison-Wesley

An imprint of Pearson Education

Boston · San Francisco · New York · Toronto · Montreal · London · Munich
Paris · Madrid · Cape Town · Sydney · Tokyo · Singapore · Mexico City

PEARSON EDUCATION LIMITED

Head Office:
Edinburgh Gate
Harlow CM20 2JE
England
Tel: +44 (0)1279 623623
Fax: +44 (0)1279 431059

London Office:
128 Long Acre
London WC2E 9AN
England
Tel: +44 (0) 20 7447 2000
Fax: +44 (0) 20 7240 5771
Website: *www.aw.com/cseng*

First published in Great Britain 2002
© TERENA 2002

The rights of TERENA and Netskills to be identified as authors of this work have been asserted by them in accordance with the Copyright, Designs and Patents Act 1988.

ISBN 0-201-75838-5

British Library Cataloguing in Publication Data
A catalogue record for this book is available from the British Library.

Library of Congress Cataloging in Publication Data
Applied for.

10 9 8 7 6 5 4 3 2 1

Translated and typeset by Land & Unwin, Bugbrooke
Printed and bound in Great Britain

The publishers' policy is to use paper manufactured from sustainable forests.

CONTENTS

PREFACE

The *Internet Users' Reference* provides a basic introduction to the Internet with sections on using email, Web browsers and searching for information. It also contains more advanced sections for those developing Web sites and needing advice on topics such as standards, security and the use of multimedia. Others services provided via the Internet are also covered, for example videoconferencing and collaborative tools.

The *Internet Users' Reference* is produced by TERENA (Trans-European Research and Education Networking Association) for the user community of its member academic and research networks. Though primarily intended for Internet users and user support staff in this community, it is made freely available via the World Wide Web to encourage and facilitate network use.

Background

The *Internet Users' Reference* was originally produced by EARN (European Academic and Research Network) under the title of *Guide to Network Resource Tools*, or GNRT. Printed as a booklet and registered in the Internet Engineering Task Force's FYI series, it became a very popular guide for end-users and support staff on using the Internet. In 1996 an update of the GNRT was started by EARN's successor, the Trans-European Research and Education Networking Association (TERENA), which resulted in a completely new version, written for the Web, covering a wide range of popular tasks and tools on the Internet today. In 2000, the second edition of a book version of this site, the *Internet Users' Guide to Network Resource Tools* was published by Addison-Wesley Longman. A separate version will be submitted as an informational RFC in the Internet Engineering Task Force's FYI series. The *Internet Users' Reference* is revised on an ongoing basis by TERENA.

Acknowledgments

This edition of the TERENA *Internet Users' Reference* was edited by Simon Hume, former Netskills Technical Trainer, and compiled and authored by the Netskills team (**netskills-admin@netskills.ac.uk**). Special thanks are due to Patris van Boxel, Helen Conroy, Chris Young, Rob Allen, Dave Hartland and all at Netskills. This edition is based on the first two editions of the GNRT which were largely authored by Margaret Isaacs **magnet@magnet-it.co.uk**. Others who have provided input to the guide include Patrick Follon, Floor Jas, Frans Ward and Roel Rexwinkel from SURFnet.

The members of the Review Panel are: Pål Axelsson (Uppsala University), Carry Böhmermann (SURFnet), Yuri Demchenko (TERENA), Debra Hiom (ILRT), Miroslav Milinovic (SRCE/CARNet).

1

WEB TOOLS

Above all other network tools, the World Wide Web has helped to advance the ongoing revolution in the use and application of networked information. It has fired the enthusiasm of users as well as the imagination of software developers, generating rapid uptake and development of new functions and capabilities. The Web has colonized most other network tools and integrated their functionality into its own all-enveloping interface to such an extent that the only essential network tool for many users is a Web browser.

In this chapter we cover:

- The World Wide Web
- Web browsers
- Web search tools
- Web search engines
- Meta-searchers
- Classified directories
- Portal services
- New developments in Web searching
- Metadata

1.1 THE WORLD WIDE WEB

The World Wide Web (WWW) is a hypermedia information system providing seamless access to distributed information on the Internet and a flexible means of publishing information.

Hypermedia

Hypermedia (or hypertext, if it is text only) documents are ones that contain embedded links (hyperlinks) to other related documents in any media. The presence of a link may be indicated to the reader by special formatting of the linked item, or some change in its appearance when the mouse is dragged over it. The information contained in the link includes the unique Internet address of the referenced document, that is, its URL (Uniform Resource Locator). The format which makes it possible to embed this information invisibly is HTML (HyperText Markup Language), the standard format for Web documents. Further details of URLs can be found in the Glossary.

When a hyperlink is selected, the document to which it refers is immediately fetched and displayed for the user. This document may contain links to further documents. Thus the user can track related concepts from one document to another, traversing the Internet in a seamless fashion, regardless of the physical location of the documents or the type of computers on which they are held.

Hyperlinking offers advantages to Web authors as well as readers. By offering optional levels of enrichment and enhancement of document content through links to related documents, it adds value and context to Web documents with an immediacy seldom possible with traditional forms of information.

Links in Web documents span not only the universe of networked information but also the range of media because the Web is a multimedia system encompassing text, audio, video, graphics and other types of information.

Distributed information

Through the WWW, the user can access documents distributed across millions of linked computers all over the world. The WWW interface makes it appear that there is one integrated corpus of documents, one massive file system, when in fact the files are held on many separate computers.

Publishing information

The WWW provides an easy, platform-independent, supremely flexible means of making information available. It is easy because Web documents are normally written in HTML, the rudiments of which are easily learnt, and for which there are many editing and conversion programs available. Documents in standard HTML can be read by any Web browser on any platform. Distribution of the information worldwide becomes just a matter of making potential users aware of it, and revision and updating of the information are managed by maintaining the files at the source of distribution, namely, on the server.

Access

Access with a client

Users access the Web with client software, normally referred to as a Web browser. There are other types of Internet client–server systems too, but with all of them the client (the browser) interacts with a remote server. The server stores the information to give out or 'publish'. The browser has the task of requesting, fetching and displaying the information on behalf of the user. Many Web browsers for different platforms are available. At the no-frills end of the spectrum are plain-text browsers such as Lynx which runs under Unix and VMS. The most popular browsers are high-end graphical browsers such as Netscape Navigator/ Communicator and Microsoft's Internet Explorer, both of which are available for PC Windows and Apple Mac. Versions of these browsers are also available for Unix.

Mosaic was the first graphical browser to gain widespread usage, but currently the bulk of Web users use either Netscape or Internet Explorer. While these two browsers are developing into massive all-encompassing Internet tools trailing plug-in and add-on programs in their wake, there is a reverse trend in specific areas such as the development of trimmed-down browsers for hand-held devices.

Standard functions of browsers

With a graphical Web browser, the user can expect to be able to:

- open desired HTML documents,
- follow links to other Web documents,
- follow links to other Internet information systems such as gopher and ftp,
- open local documents,
- save retrieved documents,
- print the current document,
- maintain a history of visited URLs,

- move back and forward between URLs visited in the current session,
- trigger programs on the server side and review the results,
- view the source (the HTML) of the current document,
- keep a note of URLs required for future reference,
- search for a term in the current document,
- handle forms,
- view images (GIF, JPEG, PNG formats) inline,
- follow links from imagemaps,
- maintain a store (cache) of visited pages for reuse where appropriate,
- configure preferences for:
  - the home (starting) page
  - the appearance of documents
  - whether or not to automatically display images
  - how particular file types should be handled
  - use of a proxy server
  - security safeguards
  - character set
  - language
  - screening access according to content rating.

Accessing a specific URL

Following embedded links in Web documents offers a convenient ready-made exploration trail. But it is also possible to tell the browser to go to a specific URL, by typing it directly into the address bar (or using the GO command with Lynx).

Additional functions of browsers

As the leading Web browsers have developed, they have absorbed more and more functions until they have arrived at a point where they effectively fill the role of all-purpose Internet tools. Email and Usenet News functionality are commonly included, plus options for chat, calendaring, Web authoring and ftp.

Offline reading of Web pages

Offline reading of Web pages enables a user to download pages, directories or even whole Web sites for reading at leisure without the expense or inconvenience of staying connected. Internet Explorer 5.0 has a facility for downloading Web pages for offline browsing.

Programs such as Webwhacker **http://www.bluesquirrel.com/products/whacker/ whacker.html** will also download pages which may be viewed offline.

Caching and caches

Retrieved Web pages may be stored (cached) locally for a time so that they can be conveniently accessed if further requests are made for them. Whether the most up-to-date copy of the file is retrieved is handled by the caching program which initially makes a brief check and compares the date of the file at its original location with that of the copy in the cache. If the date of the cached file is the same as the original, then the cached copy is used.

Web browsers maintain a cache of retrieved documents and this is used for retrievals where possible. In addition, the user may configure the browser to point to a caching server. File requests not able to be supplied from the browser cache will then be directed to the caching server. The caching server supplies the files from its cache if they are current, or passes on the request to the originating server if they are not.

Accessing the Web with telnet

The World Wide Web Consortium (W3C) has a line-mode Web browser at **telnet://telnet.w3.org/** which by default points to its own Web server. To access other Web addresses, at the prompt type the command go followed by the URL you wish to access. This facility is useful when investigating accessibility issues since it will establish a Web site's dependency upon images and graphics.

The Web protocol

A protocol in this context is a set of rules which govern the exchange of data between two computers. It is important to understand that several different protocols may be used in order to access different computers on the Internet. Different types of client software use different protocols. The main protocol of the Web is Hypertext Transfer Protocol (HTTP) – hence the familiar **http://** prefix on Web addresses. (Note: you can normally omit this prefix if you are using a reasonably up-to-date browser.)

Other Internet protocols include gopher, ftp, telnet and news, and at one time you needed different client software in order to use each different protocol. However, modern Web browsers generally have all these different functions built into them, and the user may not be aware that different protocols are being used.

Using

At a basic level, the Web offers the point and click interface for viewing documents and following hyperlinks. Viewing documents may mean reading, playing, or listening, depending on which media are included in the document and which facilities are available at the user end through the browser. Documents may include one or more files of different file types. Documents may also contain scripts or small programs which are run in response to user actions. Alternatively scripts or programs on the server may be activated through Web forms. In order to make the Web useful in a wide range of environments it supports a range of security features. These are described in Chapter 5, 'Security and encryption'.

Handling additional file types

The standard role of Web browsers is to access and display HTML documents. Browsers interpret the HTML tags and display the document accordingly. They can also retrieve and display other types of files if they recognize the Internet media type (MIME type) and have the software available to handle it. The software may be built into the browser, for example certain image file types (GIF, JPEG and PNG) are displayed by graphical browsers as an integral part of the document. Other file types may require some extra software, commonly programs designed to work in conjunction with a browser for the display of a specific file type (plug-ins), or possibly stand-alone programs which the browser can launch to handle certain file types (helper and viewer applications).

Interactivity

A Web form is a page where the user is asked to enter some data, e.g. a keyword, on which to perform a search. Web forms provide a basic level of interactivity on the Web. Through forms, input can be taken from the user, then processed in some way, and the output of the process delivered back to them. In a search engine search, for example, the Web form is used to collect search terms from the user and the data from the form is transmitted to the Web server where a script is run which sends a query to a database of index data from thousands of Web sites. The results of the database search are passed back via the server and output as a freshly generated HTML page containing the search results. The actual processing has taken place at the server end in this case.

In other cases, the interactivity is generated by the user's Web browser as it interprets scripts embedded in Web pages. These scripts or programs contain instructions for the browser on how to respond to user actions such as loading a new Web page or moving the mouse over some object on the Web page, just for visual effect. They can also be used in conjunction with forms. These 'local' scripts are more limited in what they can do, but usually the response is instantaneous – much more desirable for the user.

There are also many competing proprietary technologies used for creating multimedia/interactive Web pages. These products usually require extra plug-in software to be installed on the user's computer, to run in conjunction with the Web browser. For more detailed information, see Section 4.5 'Interactive Web pages'.

Keeping track of useful resources

With millions of resources available, identifying and finding useful material can be a problem. One important information management tool for the Web is the bookmark facility provided by Web browsers (also known as Favorites (Internet Explorer)). Bookmarks are a way of saving and organizing URLs, thus enabling users to keep track of Web resources they find useful. Most browsers provide a facility for hierarchical organization of annotated bookmarks.

EXAMPLES

The WWW is now a densely populated place and new sites proliferate at a dramatic rate. The Web has a presence in most corners of human activity, ranging from recreation to education, from scientific research to commercial transactions, and most areas in between. On the Web you can buy a house, find a job, book a cruise, check out weather maps, browse a local newspaper, look at a medieval manuscript or take a tour of the solar system. The most interesting sites are of course the ones which contain information which is pertinent to the user's interests or concerns – sites which offer solutions to problems, commercial advantage, information which is otherwise unavailable, or just plain convenience. For instance, the Web might be used to look up a list of local medical practitioners, which movies are showing in town this evening, the price of company X's shares, whether the parcel you sent today has reached its destination.

If you are interested in the techniques being used, you can see examples of the Web as frontend to a database using forms and technologies such as CGI and Active Server Pages, Flash animation, streaming audio and video and 3-D graphics. There are journals online with the look of conventionally published journals (viewed with Adobe Acrobat), interactive graphical effects produced with scripting, animated images, Java applets enhancing the interactivity of Web pages, and the use of agent technology to find a job. There is an increasing trend to relate the information on the Web to the interests and preferences of the individual.

One important and increasing trend is the use of the Web as a collaborative tool. Mailing lists and newsgroups are standard sources, but computer supported collaborative work via the Web is also possible.

Finding more information

- World Wide Web Consortium site: **http://www.w3.org/**
  The World Wide Web Consortium (W3C) is an international industry consortium which seeks to develop common standards for the evolution of the World Wide Web. These standards are issued as W3C Recommendations and supported for industry-wide adoption by Consortium members. The W3C also develops applications to demonstrate use of new technology, and a reference code implementation to embody and promote standards. It maintains a repository of information about the World Wide Web for developers and users.

- RFCs: **http://www.rfc-editor.org/rfc.html**
  RFCs (Request for Comments) are the standards developed by the working groups of the IETF (Internet Engineering Task Force). They define the protocols on which the Internet operates and constitute a primary reference source on any technical aspect of the Internet, including the WWW.

- WWW FAQ: **http://www.boutell.com/faq/**
  Maintained by Thomas Boutell and mirrored at a number of sites, the WWW FAQ (Frequently Asked Questions) answers basic questions about the Web, including information on obtaining browsers for a number of platforms such as Amiga, NeXT, VM/CMS, Acorn and others.

- Web discussion lists
  W3C Mailing lists: **http://www.w3.org/pub/WWW/Mail/Lists.html**

1.2 WEB BROWSERS

The browsers covered here are the two popular browsers from Netscape and Microsoft, as well as Opera and the plain-text browser – Lynx.

Information on other Web browsers

Yahoo!: WWW Browsers page **http://dir.yahoo.com/Computers_and_Internet/ Software/Internet/World_Wide_Web/Browsers/**

Browser Watch: **http://browserwatch.internet.com**

1.2.1 Netscape Communicator

Netscape Communicator is really a suite of software applications based around the Netscape Navigator browser. The Netscape Navigator browser supports additional technologies such as Java, JavaScript, Cascading Style Sheets and common multimedia formats.

The suite also includes an email program (Netscape Messenger), newsreader (Netscape Newsgroup), chat client (Netscape AOL Instant Messenger), and Web authoring tool (Netscape Composer). The browser includes a Flash animation viewer and optional extras such as Netscape Media Player. There are facilities for filing useful URLs (bookmarks), caching retrieved files, specification of proxies, encrypted communications and transactions (via SSL 3.0) and customizing the appearance and operation of the browser.

With recent versions, the Navigator browser incorporates a 'What's Related' feature which recommends Web sites related to the current document. Internet searches can be initiated by typing search terms into the location window. The home page of a corporation can be located by simply typing its name into the location window, e.g. 'ibm'. Offensive content can be screened out using NetWatch.

Netscape Communicator is available in European languages other than English including Danish, Italian, Portuguese, Spanish and Swedish.

Access

http://home.netscape.com /download/index.html

Platforms

System requirements for Netscape Communicator 4.5: PC with 486 or higher processor, Windows 3.x/95/98/2000/NT; Macintosh PPC System 7.6.1 or 8.1, Unix (various).

1.2.2 Microsoft Internet Explorer

Like Netscape, Internet Explorer is a suite of tools based around a Web browser. Internet Explorer (IE) supports other technologies such as Cascading Style Sheets, Java, JavaScript and various multimedia formats.

IE also supports Microsoft-specific technologies such as VBScript and ActiveX, a technology for bringing Windows-style applications to the Web. IE Version 5 also supports limited features of XML (Extended Markup Language) and its own version of downloadable fonts. Dynamic HTML is supported, and IE 5 contains a facility 'DHTML behaviors' enabling the storage of dynamic scripts independent of the pages which use them, thus providing for reusability.

IE offers a range of optional extras, including Mail and News capabilities (Outlook Express), tools for workgroup collaboration (NetMeeting), a Chat client, an ftp client, multimedia components including Windows Media Player and Macromedia Shockwave Flash, Web authoring components including FrontPage Express, and powerful multilanguage support. The appearance and operation of the browser can be customized to suit.

Convenience features introduced with the current version include AutoComplete assistance with typing in URLs, such as a prompting drop-down list of sites with similar URLs to that being typed in, and automatic correction of typos. IE5 offers added help with searching. Queries can be typed directly into the Address Bar; there is a Search Assistant to help in choosing resources to search, and a customizable Search Bar. There is a 'Related Links' option (from Alexa) to see sites like the one currently being viewed. Local secure cookies save passwords, addresses, email addresses and other details previously typed into Web forms. The data is presented in drop-down lists when a form is being filled in. Download and viewing of Web sites offline is provided for. 'File/Save as' downloads all the items that go into displaying a Web page, such as HTML, stylesheets, scripts and images.

Other language versions of IE5 are available and IE5 also supports different encodings for other alphabets, e.g Cyrillic.

Access

http://www.microsoft. com/windows/ie/default.htm

Platform

Windows 95/98/NT/2000 (versions for these platforms may be one step ahead of other platforms).

Windows 3.x, Apple Mac, Unix.

1.2.3 Opera

Like Netscape and Internet Explorer, Opera is a suite of applications based around a graphical Web browser. Opera promotes itself as an 'alternative' browser which is independent of Netscape/Microsoft, and yet offers many of the same features.

Opera is a very compact program which makes it quick to download, and it also has the advantage that it can run on older versions of Windows, e.g Windows 3.1.

Access

http://www.opera.com

Platform

Opera 4.0: Windows 3.x/95/98/NT 3.51/4, EPOC, BeOS, Linux.

1.2.4 Lynx

Lynx is a plain-text World Wide Web browser for access from character-based terminals. Lynx displays HTML documents as plain text, providing support for most common HTML tags, including plain-text rendering of tables and frames. Its functions include support for forms, menu rendering of imagemaps, caching of pages, a history function and bookmarks.

Access

http://lynx.browser.org/

Platform

Lynx 2.8.2: VMS, Unix, Windows 95/98/NT/2000, DOS via DJGPP and OS/2 EMX.

Further information on other Web browsers

http://browserwatch.internet.com/

1.3 WEB SEARCH TOOLS

The Internet has dramatically altered the information landscape and the way we search for information. With traditional printed sources, the main requirement for information searching was knowledge of where to look. With computerized bibliographic databases, the focus has shifted to the techniques for searching them: from the where to the how.

On the Internet, vast libraries of online resources and a massive array of services which index them set a scene of unprecedented information abundance in which effective searching requires both a mastery of techniques and a knowledge of sources. Thus the Internet has spawned new information industries and professions, and given researchers, educators and Internet users the world over the abiding challenge of finding useful, quality information which is pertinent to their requirements. It is no surprise then that many services have developed which try to address this need. These services help to locate specific information within the vast mass available on the World Wide Web, in Usenet News postings, in mailing list archives, and other sources.

Web search tools

Web search tools gather, index, classify and search information on the Internet. These tools are constantly being developed and improved to meet the challenge of the Web's abundance, a challenge admittedly often linked to the challenge to their own commercial survival. The benefit for users is that as techniques improve, as searching gets smarter, as more resources are classified and searchable, the chance to master the Web information environment is still on offer. The starting point is to know what the tools do and where to find them. In the following sections, we take a detailed look at the current tools. The various classes of information service, namely search engines, meta-search services, subject directories and subject gateways, are discussed and descriptive entries for a selection of each are included.

The main types of service are:

- **search engines**, which enable users to search for a specific subject in gigantic automatically generated indexes of Internet resources;
- **meta-search engines**, which enable users to search across more than one search engine simultaneously;
- **classified directories**, which select and list resources within a subject hierarchy and enable the user to browse or search these listings;
- **enhanced classified directories**, or subject gateways in which resources are evaluated and/or described by a subject expert;
- **portal services**, which aim to offer an all-round entry point to the Internet, whatever the requirements. They embrace both search engine and classified directory and usually other services as well;
- **local services, search engines, directories or gateways** that are limited to searching a specific geographic area.

Approaches to searching

Employing a variety of tactics can often be a productive strategy and portal services have quickly stepped into the breach here. They include a choice of search options from the one starting point. These options normally include a search engine, a classified directory, people and business directories, and other specialist searching facilities. Notable also as an example of throwing all the available tools at the problem are the meta-search services which enable users to search multiple indexes simultaneously. For a complex, closely specified search, the alternative approach of fine tuning can yield dividends. Mapping out the structure of the search helps to pinpoint the particular search features that will be needed. For instance, it may be obvious that Boolean searching will be required, or that only the current year's information will be useful. In these types of cases, identifying search services which offer these features is a useful exercise. Local search engines and subject catalogues are particularly useful for searching local information space.

1.4 WEB SEARCH ENGINES

Still one of the most popular starting points for finding information on the Internet is the keyword search using a Web search engine. The process can be simplicity itself but the results may be harder to deal with.

You access the search engine; type your search terms into the box provided; the search engine carries out the search and returns a list of Internet resources which appear to match your terms. You can browse through this list of hits, look at the promising ones and, if necessary, refine and re-run the search. Web search engines yield fast results and plenty of them, usually ranked according to relevance. Their databases of Web documents and other Internet resources are vast.

Getting too many results is more likely to be a problem than getting too few, though identifying the truly useful ones may require patient sifting. Many of the search engines enable advanced searching and use complex algorithms to assess the relevance of documents. Naturally, the usefulness of such techniques depends on how the user formulates the search.

In essence, Web search engines do two things:

- they gather and index data from the World Wide Web and other Internet sources;
- they provide a search facility on their index.

The programs that perform the first task are commonly referred to as robots, spiders or crawlers. They trawl through the Internet, automatically retrieving data from one site after another for inclusion in the search engine's database, possibly following a trail of hypertext links. Robots can assemble huge databases of information, but gathered indiscriminately. The database may also include manually submitted URLs.

The second element, the search facility, is accessed via a search form on a Web page. The user types a word or some words in the appropriate box describing what he or she is looking for. The search engine searches through its index database for information which seems to match what is required and returns a list of matching resources. The list of matches is usually ranked according to how well they seem to satisfy the search, and each list entry includes a hypertext link to the actual resource it references. A relevance score may also be given.

Combining search engine services with classified directory services adds a dimension of quality selection in search options. As well as a search of the huge robot-generated database, a query response may also draw on directory listings of hand-picked resources, thereby introducing a significant quality evaluation. This may be done automatically by the search engine or the user may be offered the option of searching or browsing in the relevant area of the selective classified directory.

Further potential for quality enhancement is promised by the integration of fee-based sources such as databases, journals, books and other sources with free Web data. But this phenomenon also represents a significant erosion of the 'free to the user' tradition (albeit rapidly established) of search engine services. Given the current level of dissatisfaction with the quality of content on the Web, it seems possible that we will see more of the same in the future. Relevance and ranking search engines generally produce a lot of hits. The important factor is not the volume of hits, but the relevance ranking. Do the top-ranked hits yield the answer to the user's question? This is the acid test of effectiveness. Hence search engines are turning their attention to improving search capabilities and the relevance of results rather than increasing the size of their databases. Until recently, the dominant method for assessing relevance was the frequency and location of the search terms on the Web page. Pages in which the search term(s) occurred in the title or headings and repeatedly in the text were likely to be get a higher ranking in the list of hits.

A search engine will often provide results of a very random nature. Fortunately a fresh approach which considers quality as well as words-on-the-page relevance is emerging. The quality of results can be judged in various ways. The existence of links to a site from other sites may show that it is valued, thus providing one possible index of quality. Another index is the popularity of the site. Sites preferred by users from a list of search hits and the length of time they spend perusing them may be combined to give a 'popularity' index. Another approach is to give a higher ranking to sites which have been human-selected for inclusion in a classified directory. Each of these approaches is employed in the services listed here.

Choosing a search tool

Criteria for choosing an appropriate search tool include:

- ease of use,
- comprehensiveness,
- quality of content,
- control over the search,
- flexibility in searching,
- valid assessment of relevance,
- informative presentation of results.

Ease of use

Web search services generally provide a simple entry point via a single window for input of the search term. Most search engines take the search terms and check for documents in which they are matched. Adding an extra dimension to ease of use are the search engines that are capable of analyzing and intelligently processing natural language and which can give a correct answer to a question such as 'What is the distance from London to New York?'. 'Advanced search' with its customary multiple input windows, drop-down menu selection of operators for combining search terms and specifying other parameters, may not offer the slickest of interfaces, but it provides a degree of control over the search which many users value. Quite often the same controls are available from the standard search window using rather less user-friendly devices such as AND, OR, NOT, NEAR, (), +, -, "", `fieldname:`. These methods would never make it in an 'ease of use' honors list, but in reality, they are usually used by people who like to use them, e.g. librarians.

Comprehensiveness

Many of the well-established search services index hundreds of millions of Web documents. Generally they index the full text of documents. None indexes anything like all the information on the Web, and as Web information increases, the proportion indexed decreases rather than increases. Currently, the maximum coverage by any one service is estimated at 34 percent.

Quality of content

More attention is being given by the search engines to techniques that address the issue of quality of content. Where previously speed and size were the goals, getting relevant quality search results now ranks high on the agenda of all enlightened information services. Additional processing, be it human or machine, is used to sift, sort and add value to search results. Examples of such processing are:

- subjective evaluation and rating by a human classifier;
- automatic checking of how often a resource is linked to by others;
- automatic processing of data on previous accesses to the resource.

The results of such processing, combined with matching of search terms, generates a relevance score to be used in the ranking of search results. Currency of the information in the database, particularly working links, is another aspect of quality. A number of search engines revisit URLs at variable rates depending on how often changes are made to the page.

Control over the search

In the case of complex queries, the capability for specifying search parameters in detail becomes important.

- Can you specify how multiple search terms are to be combined?

If the search engine retrieves documents containing any of the search terms, this is a different thing from retrieving documents which contain all of the terms, especially if relevance is based on a straight count of occurrences. In a search for:

```
training guide dogs blind
```

the search engine looking for documents containing any, i.e. training OR guide OR dogs OR blind, could give a higher ranking to a document containing the word training 15 times, than a document which was actually on the topic of 'Training Schools for Guide Dogs for the Blind', and contained this phrase three times. Most search engines usually allow you to specify how search terms are combined, either by typing the search string using the Boolean terms AND, OR and NOT into the search window, or giving equivalent functionality via drop-down menus. The use of parentheses in nesting Boolean search combinations provides a further level of control, e.g.

```
(cricket AND (pitch OR ground) )
```

- Can you specify whether proximity of search terms is important?
- Can you search for a phrase?

Commonly, the syntax for phrase searching, where it is provided for, is to enclose the phrase in inverted commas, for example "`formula one`".

- Can you specify which search terms must be included and which must not?

Words that must be in the document can often be indicated with a plus sign, and those to be excluded by a minus sign.

- Are words treated as words, substrings, stems?
- Does the search engine automatically truncate words?

For example, a search for `anthropologist` is interpreted as a search for `anthropolog`.

- Can you search by the word stem?

For example, `anthropolog*` to cover `anthropology`, `anthropological`, `anthropologist`, and so on.

- Is case-sensitive searching provided for?

Some search services interpret adjacent search terms starting with capital letters as proper names.

Search refinement (cascade searching)

- Can you search within the results of a previous search?
- Can you refine the search by defining the context?
- Can you add further keywords to a search already run?

Flexibility in searching

- Can a search be restricted to specific data components (fields), for example title, hosts, applets, links?
- Can the search be limited by date, in particular, for looking for recent material only?
- If you find something useful, is there the facility to search for more of the same?

- Can you search within the results of a previous search?

Assessment of relevance

- Does the search engine take quality of resources into account in ranking search results?
- Does the list of matches rank first those documents in which all the search terms were found, or is the ranking based on a raw score of occurrences of any search words in the document?
- Does the position of search terms in the document count? Frequently it is a significant factor.

Other factors that influence the ranking of search results

- Does the service sell keywords (selling of a guarantee of being found in the top ten hits for searches on a specified keyword)?
- Does the service protect itself from index spamming?

Informative presentation of results

- Are you given a total for matches found? Many search engines provide this feature.
- Do the search result entries give you enough information to judge the usefulness of following the link? Most search engines take some portion of the text to provide an abstract. Dates are often useful.
- Can the user specify alternative criteria for ranking, for example location, date?
- Is site grouping an option? A number of search engines give the option of treating all pages from one site as one entry, a feature which is often useful.
- Do the links to search results work? i.e. how current is the search engine's index database?

Index spamming

Index spamming is the practice of inappropriately stacking Web pages with words likely to be used as search terms and hence boosting the chances of being found through a search and accessed. Index terms may be incorporated into the metadata in the head of the document or placed in an area of the document body not normally seen by the user. Some search engines have built-in safeguards against index spamming and may block offending sites.

Further information on search engines

Search Engine Watch: **http://www.searchenginewatch.com**

1.4.1 AltaVista

AltaVista is an index searcher offering fast and flexible searching of a very large Internet database.

Access

http://www.altavista.com

AltaVista has established several regional sites including the USA, Canada, the UK, France, Germany, Sweden and the Netherlands and has created many other partnerships with sites around the world. A text-only interface is available.

Coverage

AltaVista is a portal site. In addition to its search engine, it offers specialty searches, a hierarchically classified directory of subject resources, news, and other services such as free email and an instant translation service. Its specialty searches include searches for images, audio and video. Searches can also be restricted to the Web, news sites, discussion groups or products. AltaVista also has several subject content sites, covering topics such as travel, money, sports, entertainment and travel.

AltaVista's classified directory offers a hierarchical path to lists of selected resources grouped by subject. There is also the option of a keyword search on the directory that will generate a list of relevant directory categories as well as hits.

AltaVista's searching facility accesses not only its own database generated from full-text indexing of many millions of Web documents and other Internet sources, but also the 'answer database' licensed from AskJeeves. This database contains the answers to millions of common questions. AltaVista's own index is updated daily with new material. Existing entries are revisited according to the frequency at which they appear to change. Manually submitted URLs are added in on a daily basis.

AltaVista offers the option of framing the search in any one of 25 languages and also limiting the search results by language. Its translation services can be used to translate Web pages text to or from English, French, German, Italian, Spanish and Portuguese.

Using

AltaVista offers natural language searching using the AskJeeves technology and database, enabling users to frame a question as they would say it, e.g. 'What is the distance from London to New York?' It also offers search refinement, which enables the user to specify which of the relevant terms are required and which should be excluded. The option of Advanced Search for specialized searches remains, with the facilities for Boolean searching (using AND, OR, AND NOT with search terms), nested search terms, and date-limited searches (e.g. only after 1/1/1999).

Advanced search

Complementing the natural language searching in the basic search, AltaVista offers some extra facilities for exercising control over the search:

- phrases can be indicated with the use of quotes, for example "`nuclear diffusion reactor`";
- words which must be included in results can be indicated with a '+' and those to be excluded with a '–';
- searches can be restricted to specific types of information (field) such as applets, hosts, domains, images or links, or title. For example, to search for sites which link to the *TERENA Guide to Network Resource Tools*, run a search on link:

  `www.terena.nl/gnrt`

- searching on a word stem is possible, for example `librar*`;
- a good help facility is provided.

In response to a search, a list of matched items ranked in order of relevance is returned. Where the question and answer are recorded in the 'answer database', the response can be very precise and relevant without further searching. Otherwise, the relevance of a document is determined by:

- how many of the search terms the page contains;
- where the words are in the document (ranked higher if in first few words);
- how close to each other they are.

AltaVista automatically clusters Web results by site, so that only one page from each site appears. However, the option is provided to view the other pages from a particular site if desired.

Finding more information

AltaVista provides a detailed Help file for both Simple and Advanced queries, as well as pages for specialty searches.

1.4.2 AskJeeves

AskJeeves is a natural language search service underpinned by a knowledge base of millions of answers to the most popular questions asked online. It also provides a meta-search option that delivers answers from five other search engines. AskJeeves works by analyzing the words and structure of a question and then searching through a database to find an appropriate answer.

Access

http://www.ask.com

The technology and database have been implemented in AltaVista, Dell's customer support system, AskDudley, and other systems. A UK site was recently launched at **http://www.ask.co.uk**

Coverage

AskJeeves runs queries against its proprietary KnowledgeBase and supplements this with a metasearch on five leading search engines. Its KnowledgeBase of popular questions and answers does not merely match text strings, but is able to differentiate word meanings, and analyze word usage in context. The KnowledgeBase has been built up through survey and analysis of the most asked questions on the Web over a number of years. As it expands, the claim is that it gets smarter.

Using

AskJeeves performs very well with standard popular questions, such as ones on measures, distances, demographic details, and so on. Questions can be phrased in plain, simple English without having to use keywords or Boolean search strings. AskJeeves carries out its own processing on the meaning and grammar of the question, then asks for confirmation to make sure it has understood the question correctly. Upon confirmation, it aims to link directly to relevant, high quality answers. The emphasis is on producing a concise list of answers with their exact location rather than an exhaustive list of matches. The simple user-friendly interface belies the complexity of the search technology behind it. Nor does it complicate the interface by allowing for definition of parameters in the additional meta-search option. If specific controls over the search are required, such as choice of languages in AltaVista, it is necessary to go to the search engine itself.

1.4.3 Excite

Excite is a portal site with a full text Web search engine. It offers personalization of its opening page with customized views of news, weather, stocks, sports, services, chat forums. The classified directory (using Magellan) lists selected resources within broad subject areas such as Autos, Careers, Shopping, Sports and Travel. Completing the picture of an all-round portal, Excite offers services such as People Finder, Stock Quotes, Weather reports, Excite Communities, Chat, etc. Note that the layout and services offered varies between the main US site and regional sites.

Still integral to its usefulness, however, is the search engine featuring its own concept-based architecture. One of its features is the use of statistical techniques in the assessment of relevance: that is, it looks not just at the number of times that words occur in documents, but also at where they occur relative to one another and their position in the document.

Access

http://www.excite.com

Excite has sites in Australia, France, Germany, Italy, Japan, Netherlands, Sweden and the UK presented in the language of the country. It also has a site in Chinese.

Coverage

The Excite search engine is a full text searcher of tens of millions of Web sites, and thousands of newsgroups. The Excite Directory is a descriptive catalogue of some thousands of Web sites selected on the basis of quality. Searches can be run on the whole of the Web database, the Directory, or a category within the Directory. Search results are not limited to just Web pages: results can include relevant information including stock quotes, sports scores, weather reports, company information, and headline news.

Using

A notable feature of Excite's service is its concept-based searching. As well as searching for the exact words specified in the query, Excite expands the search to look for closely linked words. Its Help document cites this example:

> Suppose you enter 'elderly people financial concerns' in the query box. In addition to finding sites containing those exact words, the spider will find sites mentioning the economic status of retired people and the financial concerns of senior citizens.

Searches for specific terms work best and the results are sorted by relevance. The regional Excite sites allow searches to be restricted to region or country, e.g. Europe, UK, from the main search page. Excite also offers the refining feature called the Search Wizard which will suggest additional words to add to your search if desired.

To search for a particular phrase, the phrase should be placed in quotes, e.g. "old age pension". A plus sign before a search term indicates that it is required in documents retrieved. A minus sign indicates that it must not be included, e.g. +pension -accommodation.

Keywords can be combined with Boolean operators and syntax. Boolean operators such as AND, OR, NOT must be expressed in upper case. Combinations of search terms can be grouped using parentheses, for example:

```
(schools OR training) AND guide AND dogs AND blind
```

1.4.4 FAST (alltheweb.com)

FAST (alltheweb.com) is a search engine which aims to have the largest index on the Web. FAST also has separate indexes for ftp files, MP3 files, multimedia files and various other resources.

Access

http://www.alltheweb.com

Using

Search syntax can be used, e.g. " " around phrases, + before terms which must be included and – before terms which must be excluded.

The advanced search provides additional options such as language specification, additional words to include or exclude, URLs to include or exclude, and the number of results to display. There is also a result restrictions function allowing reduction of offensive content. Unlike other search engines the FAST software doesn't avoid stop words such as: to, be, or, not. So, it is possible to search for "to be or not to be".

Finding more information

To find out about all the services offered at FAST and advice on how to use them see: **http://www.ussc.alltheweb.com/help**

1.4.5 Google

Google is a relatively new search engine that was developed as a research project at Stanford University. It is described as a 'next-generation' search engine in that it uses a completely different ranking method to that used by conventional search engines such as AltaVista. Rather than use criteria such as the number of times a search term appears on a page, Google uses its own PageRank technology to rank sites. This uses the link structure of the Web to determine the quality of a Web site – a site is judged to be a quality site if a lot of other sites link to it from their own sites. This method is usually referred to as 'link popularity'.

Access

http://www.google.com

Coverage

Google is one of the largest search engines around, indexing over a billion pages. However, because Google makes use of link data, it can return results that it has not actually indexed (they have been linked to by an indexed page) and so can potentially retrieve many more sites than it actually indexes. Google has recently added a directory service. This takes listings from the Open Directory and applies the PageRank technology to determine how they are listed within Google. In most classified directories, sites are listed within categories alphabetically, potentially giving an advantage to those sites that come early in the alphabet. Google therefore provides a solution to this problem.

Using

Google has a very clear interface, the focal point being the search box. Simply enter a term in the search box and press the Google Search button. Alternatively, the button called 'I'm Feeling Lucky' will take you directly to the Web site of the first result on your list, rather than retrieving the full results listing.

After pressing the Google Search button, results that match your search terms will be retrieved and ranked according to the PageRank of the individual sites. A site will be given a high PageRank if it has a lot of other sites linking to it. If one of the sites that links to a particular result itself has a high PageRank, this is judged to be more significant.

For all the pages that Google has indexed, the results page contains a link to a 'cached' page, which provides a copy of the page as it was when it was indexed. This can be useful if a particular site is unavailable or if the information has changed on the existing page. Each search result also has a link to the GoogleScout, which is Google's version of the 'more like this' or 'find similar' facility found in other search engines.

Advanced searching

Google provides facilities for searching on domain, language, links and specific topics. It also has other advanced searching and provides the option of using + to include words, – to exclude words and " " to specify phrases. If more than one word is entered in a search, Google automatically searches for both (an 'AND' search). It does not provide facilities for truncating words and there is no way to perform an 'OR' search.

Finding more information

See Google's search help page at **http://www.google.com/help.html**

1.4.6 HotBot

HotBot is a portal service that is part of the Lycos Network. It offers a powerful search engine from Inktomi plus information resources in categories such as news, sports, reference, travel, shopping, finance, jobs, business, education, computers, Web development. HotBot currently uses the Open Directory as its associated directory. There are options to search discussion groups, White Pages and Yellow Pages and other sources. It also offers free email accounts and home pages.

Access

http://hotbot.lycos.com

Coverage

HotBot indexes words, links and media files on more than 110 million Web documents and refreshes its database of documents every three to four weeks. HotBot provides a window in which to type search terms and a number of drop-down menus for the definition of further search parameters. Using more search terms helps to focus the search more precisely. These are some of the available options:

- `all of the words/any of the words/exact phrase/page title/ person/links` to this URL/Boolean phrase;
- time span options ranging from `'in the last week'` up to `'in the last two years'` or `'anytime'`;
- number of results;
- full descriptions/brief descriptions/URLs only.

Additional options on the Advanced Search page allow the user to specify:

- words which must or must not be contained,
- a starting date for the date range,
- media types which must be on the page,
- domain,
- page depth,
- word stemming.

Search results give the ranked hits from HotBot's database with a relevance score, links to partner sites, and also a link to the most visited sites for these search terms, using Direct Hit's popularity index. This last item is a significant step away from complete reliance on words-on-the-page relevance ranking. Direct Hit measures popularity by 'click-through data', i.e. analysis of records of user selections from search results and the length of time spent perusing the pages selected.

Finding more information

http://hotbot.lycos.com/help/

1.4.7 GO

GO is produced by Infoseek and Disney and offers a portal site strategically aimed at areas of mass appeal. A range of information services such as ABCNEWS.com for news, ESPN.com for sports, Disney.com and Family.com for kids and family, and ABC.com for entertainment, bring their specializations under the GO umbrella. At the heart of the service is the search engine, which like other established search engines, has a very large database and fast and flexible searching. It employs intelligent features for improving the accuracy and effectiveness of searching.

Access

http://www.go.com

In addition to the portal site at this address, there are a number of international partner sites (link at the bottom of the page) which concentrate on regional content.

Coverage

GO includes an enormous index comprising some tens of millions of unique URLs, of which the majority are full-text indexed. The integrity of the database is supported by a process of elimination of dead links and duplicate pages and its currency is maintained by real-time indexing. GO seeks to align its frequency of re-indexing of Web sites with the frequency at which pages change.

The GO network offers topic-specific 'centers' for business, careers, computer, entertainment, Internet, kids, money, news, sports, travel, etc. These centers consist of a collection of resources on the subject and center-specific searching. Sites in the classified GO Guides are hand-picked for their quality and given a star rating.

The site also provides personalized entry page, reference services such as White Pages, Yellow Pages, Email lookup, dictionary, translator, maps, chat forums, complementing the traditional search engine. Using natural language searching is possible and special search expressions are also allowed.

Using

Standard searches return a list of matches consisting of the relevant classification headings from the GO Guides directory and hits from the Internet database. An index of relevance is given with each hit, as well as the option to 'Find similar pages'. The default ranking is by relevance, but results can also be sorted by date. There is also the option to group all hits from the one site together. A useful feature is the facility to search within search results. Advanced search options also offer the facility to restrict searches to the Web, news, companies, newsgroups, stocks etc. The international sites offer the option of searching within the region for that site, or the Web as a whole.

In addition to the Advanced Search which features drop-down menus for defining search parameters, there are a number of ways in which the standard search can be more closely specified. The use of capitalized search terms indicates to the search engine that these are proper names. Phrases may be indicated by quotation marks, for example:

```
"guide dogs"
```

Required search terms can be denoted with a plus sign, and terms to be rejected with a minus sign, for example:

```
"guide dogs" +blind -deaf
```

GO attempts to interpret search terms intelligently. For instance, it automatically recognizes proper names and phrases. It will extend a search to cover variant forms of a given word, for example:

```
CDROM, CD-ROM, CD ROM
```

Using GO's field syntax, it is possible to confine the search to URLs, sites, titles or hypertext links. For example, to search for sites which include links to the TERENA Web server, the search terms would be:

```
link:http://www.terena.nl/
```

Commas can be used to separate names and titles.

1.4.8 Lycos

There are many regional versions of Lycos available around the world and they vary in their layout and functionality. Some Lycos sites, mainly the US site (**http://www.lycos.com**) and other sites based in the Americas function primarily as classified directories, whereas most of the European Lycos sites carry on functioning primarily as search engines. This section will focus on using the search engine based sites.

At the directory-based Lycos sites, the results returned from a search have come from a Web catalogue provided by the Open Directory. This is a directory compiled by thousands of volunteer Web editors. It is becoming an increasingly popular service, providing Web listings to many search tools; as well as Lycos, Open Directory listings are used at AltaVista, HotBot and Google. More information on the Open Directory can be found at **http://www.dmoz.org/**

The Lycos search engine used at other sites provides searching of a large robot-generated database. In addition to the search engine, Lycos offers additional services such as a classified directory of selected and rated Web sites (Webguides), specialist searching, and a range of other services such as free email and WWW home pages, chat services, newsgroups, news, etc.

Access

http://www.lycos.co.uk

There are Lycos sites in several countries around the world – links to all available regional sites can be found at the bottom of any Lycos home page. Users are automatically redirected to their nearest site.

Coverage

The Lycos search engine database indexes some tens of millions of Web pages, and other specialist directories add substantially to the subject base. Searches can be run on the Web, on sound and picture files in the database, on regional resources, businesses, books, etc. 'Webguides' include subject listings of Mini-Guides, Top Ten resources and Other Resources.

Using

The standard Lycos search is accessed from a simple search window into which search terms are typed. When the search results are returned, they are automatically clustered by domain, so that the URL of a site is displayed followed by the pages from that site which match your search terms. At the bottom of the page, there is the option to refine the search. Search refinement allows the user to specify how the search terms should be combined, for instance using AND or OR, their adjacency, degree of proximity or whether they should be treated as a phrase. If further options are required, there is a link to 'All Search Options' which provides menus for every possible parameter available within Lycos, e.g.

- whether the entire document is to be searched or just its title or URL and whether the search is to be confined to a selected Web site;

- the language to be used;
- factors most relevant to this search such as the inclusion of all the search terms, their frequency or position within the document;
- how the results should be displayed.

Finding more information

Under the Help heading in the left sidebar there are links to explanations on Search Options, Relevancy, Boolean. There is also a Help link beside the search window.

1.4.9 Northern Light

Northern Light is a search engine which aims to encompass not just Web material but also quality material in databases, magazines and other sources not normally on open access on the Internet. It employs a unique strategy of dynamically organizing search results into folders.

Access

http://www.northernlight.com

Coverage

Nothern Light is one of the biggest search engines, currrently indexing over 200 million Web pages. It also indexes the full text of many recent journal articles, plus reviews, books, databases and news wires. These 'special collections', of which there are more than 6000, include titles such as *American Banker, ENR: Engineering News Record*, *The Lancet*, *PR Newswire*, and ABC, NPR, and Fox News Transcripts. Most sources include articles back to January 1995.

Using

Content of the special collection is fully searchable and integrated with the Web. When multiple search terms are keyed in, Northern Light returns hits of all types in which most of the search terms are present. Results are ranked by relevance, and at the same time, a parallel process of organizing the results into folders based on subject, document type, source and language takes place. This process is not unlike having a hierarchical classified directory structure dynamically generated from the search results. As with a classified directory, this facilitates drilling down to specific subsets of the topic. As you navigate down or up the hierarchy of folders (i.e. narrowing or broadening the search), you can see a graphical representation of the classification and relative position of the results currently displayed. The search engine supports Boolean searching, phrase searching, word stemming and field searching. Power Search allows for specifying additional options including:

- where in the document the search terms should be looked for (anywhere/title/ name/URL),
- date range,
- sources,
- subjects,
- type of document.

Summaries of items in the 'Special Collection' are included in search results and are free. These are in the form of a standardized entry with basic information about the item. The actual articles must be purchased and can be viewed as soon as payment is made via a secure online credit card transaction. Prices range from $1 to $4 per article.

Finding more information

Northern Light provides Help pages on the site. For details on the Special Collections, see: **http://www.northernlight.com/docs/specoll_help_overview.html**

1.5 META-SEARCHERS

What are they?

Meta-search services (or metacrawlers) offer simultaneous searching of a number of search engines from one starting point. When the user keys in some search terms, the meta-searcher runs the search request on a number of associated search engines, and collects the results. It may then select from the results, process them and generate a composite list of hits, representing, in theory, the best matches from a range of search engines. It may then carry out some further processing of the results, for example allocating an overall relevance score, sorting by relevance or other criteria, formatting in a consistent manner, verifying availability and removing redundant URLs. The final list of results will be a collective list which usually indicates which search engine generated which entries. Possibly it might be grouped according to the originating search engine.

Pros and cons

In a situation where there are many different search engines to choose from, none of which is perfect or comprehensive, and where the use of multiple approaches and tools to find information is a frequently recommended strategy, meta-search services would appear to hold out the promise of the ideal all-purpose solution. They have developed sophisticated searching and processing operations in order to monitor the performance and results of multiple simultaneous searches. But the task of generating and post-processing searches from a number of search engines and returning results within an acceptable time is an ambitious undertaking. So much relies on the effectiveness and speed of services over which there is no direct control, that it is not surprising that there are some trade-offs.

Functionality

These are some of the functions meta-search services should be able to perform:

- merge search results from a number of search engines and eliminate duplicates;
- use their own query language, though this means that some of the special capabilities of some search engines will be lost;
- deal in manageable quantities of information. This means a built-in cut-off point on search results which sometimes gives a surprisingly brief list of results;
- customize the search engines that are used. Most have a default selection but increasingly customization is being supported.

Quality

The quality of the results ultimately relies on the indexing and searching capabilities of the search engines used. If even one of them generates rubbish, it will degrade the quality of the meta-searcher's results.

Control

Search engines use different search algorithms, and with a generic request there is not the same potential for close specification of the search, nor for further refinement.

Speed

If results are being presented as one integrated list, one slow search engine can impose delays on the display of all results. The meta-searchers have looked for ways around these problems. For instance MetaCrawler incorporates a mechanism for verifying that items in the collective list of search results are actually accessible and are relevant to the search before displaying them. In selecting which search engines to use for a search, Search.com takes into account the current turn-around time for each search engine and gives preference to those which are faster.

1.5.1 MetaCrawler

MetaCrawler is a Web search service which searches several Web search engines simultaneously and returns a composite list of results. It is a search engine of search engines.

Access

http://www.metacrawler.com

Metacrawler is managed by InfoSpace.

Coverage

MetaCrawler has no database of its own but relies on the databases of the sources it uses. The general Web search at Go2Net includes AltaVista, Excite, Infoseek, Lycos, WebCrawler, Yahoo!, Thunderstone, LookSmart, About.com, Google, GoTo.com, Direct Hit and RealNames. Searches can be run on the Web (using the general Web search engines), the MetaCrawler directory (provided by the Open Directory), Audio/MP3 files, Newsgroups (using Deja.com) and Auctions.

Using

MetaCrawler provides a single search window from which a search on multiple search engines is generated. When keying in search terms, users can specify whether they want hits which include any of the search terms, all of them or to have the search terms treated as a phrase. They can search the Web, Directory, Audio/MP3, Newsgroups or Auctions. MetaCrawler reports on the search as it carries it out and collates the search results into a single uniformly formatted list, eliminating duplicate URLs and verifying that the items in the list are accessible and relevant to the search. By default, search results are listed in order of relevance, with the confidence score given to each reference by the originating search engines taken into account in the ranking. In search engine searches, advanced search syntax can be used, e.g. " " around phrases, + before terms which must be included, – before terms which must be excluded.

Advanced search

The Power Search option provides additional options such as selecting the engines to use, a timeout period, how many results to display etc.

Finding more information

To find out about all the services offered at MetaCrawler and advice on how to use them see:

http://www.metacrawler.com/help/faq/

1.5.2 Search.com

Search.com is a meta-search tool which provides fast simultaneous querying of multiple Internet search engines and other sources, and integration and display of result sets.

Access

http://www.search.com

Coverage

Search.com has over 800 resources for use in meta-searches, including:

- search engines, e.g. Excite, AltaVista, HotBot,
- classified directories, e.g. Yahoo!, Mining Co, Magellan, LookSmart,
- Usenet, e.g. Deja.com,
- shareware, e.g. Jumbo, TUCOWS, Shareware.com,
- email addresses, e.g. Yahoo! People Search, UsenetAddresses,
- newspapers, e.g. New York Times,
- encyclopedias, e.g. Encyclopedia Britannica, Encarta,
- travel, e.g. CIA World Factbook, Lonely Planet,
- movies, e.g. Internet Movie Database.

Using

Search.com offers a general meta-search using the user's choice of either search engines, classified directories (called Guides by Search.com), Usenet News, news or shareware. When a query is submitted, Search.com assesses which search tools will most efficiently provide an answer and runs the search on these first. By default it looks for documents which contain all the search terms in the query unless the option of treating them as a phrase has been selected. The results are integrated and listed, each descriptive entry indicating which search tool(s) generated that result. If the results are not satisfactory, the search can be re-run using a further group of search tools.

There are also specialty meta-searches in areas such as domain names, email addresses, education, encyclopedias, health, images, investing, jobs, magazine articles, movies, travel, etc. In addition 'shop' collections offer comparison meta-shopping. The search customization feature enables users to define their own meta-search. From Search.com's 800+ search resources, users can choose the ones they wish to use, rank the importance of each, give the customized meta-search a name, and have it listed as an additional specialty option whenever they access Search. Search.com offers structured queries when the option of using either search engines or classified directories has been selected. The query language supports phrase searching (" "), enforced term operators (+/–), Boolean language (AND, OR, NOT) and nested searches using parentheses. Search.com will assess which search engines or directories can handle the query. Search.com's query page is available in more than 20 languages.

Finding more information

Search.com help FAQ: **http://www.search.com/help/index.html**

1.6 CLASSIFIED DIRECTORIES

Classified directories are catalogues of resources that have been selected and evaluated by humans. (Records are usually created for resources which sometimes contain a description and perhaps keywords.) The resources are then organized to allow structured browsing and searching.

Classified directories (or subject directories) offer a selection of broad subject divisions at the top level, from which to begin a search. Making increasingly specific choices takes you down through the subject hierarchy. Classified directories offer the benefit of grouping like with like, enabling you to see individual resources in their broader subject context. And because the resources are human-selected, there is likely to be a better chance of locating quality information than with a search engine. The disadvantage of this approach is that you cannot always predict how a subject will be classified. Thus your descent through the hierarchy may lead to a dead-end. The fall-back position (or possibly the preferred approach) is to use the search facility which most classified directories provide. When searching a classified directory, however, it is important to remember you are searching the 'catalogue record' created for that resource, not the full text of the resource itself. Some classified directories also include abstracts or reviews, which can be very useful in sifting through long lists of resources.

Subject gateways are simply classified directories that are devoted to one specific subject.

In looking for the appropriate tool for a search, it may be useful to note that classified directories usually have the following features:

- **Context-based searching**   As in a library arranged by subject, items are arranged with like items, and lateral browsing may offer fruitful possibilities.
- **Selected resources**   Selectivity may well compensate for lack of compre- hensiveness in some cases, for instance, in searching for a standard or classic work in a subject area.
- **Improved chance of finding quality resources**   Even though many items may be self-selected by their authors, many will also have been selected for inclusion because they have been found useful by others.
- **Low risk of duplication and redundancy**   In contrast to automatic index searching, selective human-compiled lists will not normally throw up multiple hits for the same work.

Subject organization

One disadvantage of using a classified directory is that you cannot always predict how a subject will be classified. The system of subject organization may be no system at all but the ad hoc creation of the authors such as at Yahoo!, or it may be a standard library classification scheme such as UDC (Universal Decimal Classification). Standard library classification schemes offer the benefits of greater consistency and widespread recognition and acceptance.

Added value

Classified directories are a useful complement to search engines, where, frequently, individual entries are lacking in detail, and may in fact be just a URL. Listings with annotations or descriptive entries provide more information about the resources listed and increase their potential for usefulness. Unlike search engines, these entries are human-generated rather than machine-generated and may in some cases include an evaluation of quality. Entries may be formally structured and use a standard list of fields, much like a library catalogue entry.

1.6.1 Yahoo!

Yahoo! is a classified directory that has developed into a portal site offering a collection of services, the core of which is the one for which it is famous – its classified directory of resources. This was a pioneer service of its type on the Internet and it continues to lead the field. It is one of the most popular services on the Web, offering the reassurance that all the resources it lists have been pre-selected and classified by a person rather than an automated robot, and at the same time providing the choice and diversity that comes with a substantial collection of resources. Complementing its browsable directory is a flexible search facility.

Access

http://www.yahoo.com

There are European sites for Yahoo! in Denmark, France, Germany, Italy, Norway, Spain, Sweden and the UK; sites in the Americas and the Pacific Rim, and also a number of local Yahoos.

Coverage

The Yahoo! directory lists many thousands of resources within its hierarchy of subject categories. At the top of the hierarchy are 14 broad headings such as Arts & Humanities, Business & Economy, Computers & Internet, Education, Science, Society & Culture. Underneath each of these is a hierarchy of subject subdivisions, and within these are the entries for resources classed under the subject. The hyperlinked entries may consist of title only, or title and a brief description. Some entries have hyperlinks to reviews of that resource or an icon denoting good presentation or content.

Using

Yahoo! can be browsed or searched but its great strength is its subject-based listings and the associated opportunity of browsing resources in a specific area. The great value of the search facility in this context is as a tool to find Web sites organized by subject rather than as a tool to find specific Web sites.

Browsing

Browsing starts at one of the 14 broad topics at the top level, then proceeds down through the subject hierarchy to reach the desired topic. For example, a user might select the top level category of Business and Economy, then proceed to the next level where there are links to general works on the subject such as Directories and Indices, to further subcategories, and to any actual titles in this category. The number of entries within each subcategory is shown in brackets beside it. Following a subcategory link leads to a further similar listing.

Searching from inside the directory

When browsing in the Yahoo! directory, at any point there is the option to search the current category or Yahoo! as a whole. Subject hierarchies can be very extensive and deep, so the Search facility is a necessary adjunct. Search results are listed under their Yahoo! category. This usefully provides a link to the category and the other resources listed there. This demonstrates one of the advantages of subject classified directories, namely that they allow the user to see resources within their subject context, whether working from the top down, or the bottom up.

General search

The general search facility (available from the Home Page) offers searches on Yahoo! subject categories and Web sites plus a general Web search. The search generates a summary of best matches from each area. Results are ranked by relevance measured by the number of search words matched, exact word matches, and location of the matched words in the document (location in title ranks higher). The first set of results are Yahoo! categories. A category can contain hundreds or even thousands of relevant Web sites. If no categories are found, Yahoo! goes on to show the next set of results (Web sites). These are sites found in the Yahoo! directory which are listed with the categories that contain them. If no Yahoo! sites are found, it goes on to the next set of results (Web pages) generated from a full-text Web search by the Inktomi search engine. An Advanced Search option is also available which offers extras such as searching Usenet News

(DejaNews) or Yahoo!. Searches can be limited to the last day, week, month, year or three years. Search terms can be joined with AND or OR, and regarded as a substring or a complete word.

Finding more information

Yahoo! How-To: **http://howto.yahoo.com**

FAQ: **http://www.yahoo.com/docs/info/faq.html**

Yahoo! Search Help: **http://help.yahoo.com/help/ysearch/**

1.6.2 Subject gateways

There are a number of services which bring subject expertise to bear on the selection, classification and description of resources. These subject gateways select, classify and describe quality resources in a specified subject area. They effectively fill the role of information broker for information seekers in that subject, and the people selecting and describing resources are usually subject specialists, for example librarians. These gateways can be relied on to identify useful quality online resources, and to be an important resource for anyone working in a field in which there is a significant mass of online source material.

Examples of subject gateways

- BIZ/ED: **http://www.bized.ac.uk** Lists selected quality resources in business and economics.
- EEVL: **http://www.eevl.ac.uk** Searchable catalogue of reviews and links to quality engineering Web sites, engineering search engines, indexes to print literature and other specialist information services.
- HUMBUL: **http://www.humbul.ac.uk** Humanities resources.
- OMNI: **http://www.omni.ac.uk** UK's gateway to quality biomedical Internet resources.
- Australia's Cultural Network: **http://www.acn.net.au**
- PICK: **http://www.aber.ac.uk/~tplwww/e/** Gateway to quality librarianship and information science resources.
- The Social Science Information Gateway (SOSIG): **http://www.sosig.ac.uk** Provides a quality-controlled listing of online resources in social sciences and related areas. Each resource listed is described and classified using a standard entry template.

Collections of subject gateways

- Pinakes Subject Launchpad: **http://www.hw.ac.uk/libWWW/irn/pinakes/ pinakes.html** Based at Heriot-Watt University, this site brings together links to mainly UK-based academic subject gateways.
- WWW Virtual Library: **http://www.vlib.org/Home.html** The pioneer of quality subject listings, the well-recognized Virtual Library is run by a loose confederation of volunteers, who compile pages of key links for particular areas in which they are expert.
- InfoMine Scholarly Academic Resource Collections: **http://infomine.ucr.edu/** Classified descriptive listing of useful Internet/Web resources including databases, electronic publications, mailing lists, library catalogues and so on.
- The Scout Report Archives: **http://scout.cs.wisc.edu/archives/** A searchable and browsable database to over five years' worth of the Scout Reports and subject-specific Scout Reports giving access to over 10,000 Internet sites and mailing lists.
- AlphaSearch: **http://www.calvin.edu/library/searreso/internet/as/** The primary purpose of AlphaSearch is to access the finest Internet 'gateway' sites. The authors of these gateway sites have spent significant time gathering into one place all relevant sites related to a discipline, subject or idea.

In the UK, a federation of subject gateways is being created as part of the Resource Discovery Network. Maintenance of gateways is being rationalized to create subject 'hubs' which will have broader subject coverage, for example BIOME at **http://biome.ac.uk** will be the hub for Health and Life Sciences and will subsume the existing OMNI medical gateway. For further information on the Resource Discovery Network see **http://www.rdn.ac.uk**

1.7 PORTAL SERVICES

An increasing trend is to host a whole collection of services together under the one umbrella and present it as a 'total' information solution. In addition to the basic search engine and classified directory, such umbrella services offer facilities such as finding email and postal addresses, finding telephone and fax numbers, locating details of companies, getting share prices, reading current news and weather reports, online shopping, free email accounts and home pages. In this way they seek to fulfill the role of main entry point to the Internet, i.e. to be an

Internet portal, whatever the user's information needs. Examples of portal services include:

- AltaVista: **http://www.altavista.com**
- Excite: **http://www.excite.com**
- HotBot: **http://www.hotbot.com**
- Go/InfoSeek: **http://infoseek.go.com**
- Lycos: **http://www.lycos.com**
- MSN: **http://www.msn.com**
- Netscape NetCenter: **http://www.netcenter.com**
- Yahoo!: **http://www.yahoo.com**

Of the portal services, AltaVista, Excite, HotBot, Go/Infoseek and Lycos started out as search engine services and have gone on to supplement the basic search facility with a whole range of additional services. Yahoo! began life as a classified directory but its alliance with the search engine Inktomi allows it to offer a similar all-round service to the other portals, and they in turn, offer classified directory services too. Some include evaluations of listed resources, e.g. Go/Infoseek and Lycos.

Customized information retrieval

'Personalized' services are now being offered by many portals. These allow users to tailor their own home pages, delivering news stories, stock prices, weather reports, horoscopes etc. all selected by the user. Examples of services that can be personalized are:

- Yahoo!: **http://my.yahoo.com/?myHome**
- AltaVista Live!: **http://live.altavista.com**

'Push technologies' deliver customized information to the desktop, allowing the user to get on with other tasks while information is delivered to them. EntryPoint at **http://www.entrypoint.com** delivers information either as a screensaver or on a toolbar that is constantly on the desktop.

Taking this model further, **intelligent agents** (see Section 1.8.2) will hopefully learn about our information needs and go out there and find information for us, without us having to do too much at all.

1.8 NEW DEVELOPMENTS IN WEB SEARCHING

The sheer amount of information on the Web and the difficulties involved in finding relevant information means that there is a constant quest to improve searching and so search tools are becoming more and more sophisticated. Developments are being made in several areas, attacking the problem of effective information retrieval from different angles. Some approaches involve developing technologies to deal with the existing state of information on the Web, whereas other approaches involve addressing more fundamental problems of information organization, and attempt to develop models for structuring information on the Web.

1.8.1 Advances in search engine technology

Existing search engines are continuing to add more features, such as suggesting related keywords or searches. More sophisticated ranking algorithms are being used, incorporating new criteria such as link popularity or user popularity. The search engine Google **http://www.google.com** bases its whole ranking method on link popularity. The Direct Hit service **http://www.directhit.com** describes itself as a 'popularity engine'. It works alongside existing search engines such as HotBot and monitors user searches, looking at what users search for, which sites they go to and how long they stay there. Direct Hit then compiles a Top Ten of the most popular sites related to particular search terms. Another search engine variation is Oingo which uses a database of over one million words and meanings, linked by millions of relationships, to try and refine the search to what it refers to as a 'meaning based search'.

New methods of searching will continue to be developed by existing search tools and brand new tools will continue to be developed. To keep up to date on search engine developments visit the Searchenginewatch site: **http://searchenginewatch.com** or subscribe to their newsletter at: **http://www.searchenginewatch.com/sereport/index.html**

See also 'Customized Information Retrieval' above and Sections 1.8.2 and 1.9 below.

1.8.2 Intelligent agents

Agents (software agents) are programs which carry out tasks on behalf of users. The spectrum of capability of agents is wide, ranging from the basic level of automating straightforward routine tasks through to the ability to adapt to user routines and preferences, and even to negotiate on behalf of users. The feature that distinguishes intelligent agents from other programs is the ability to automatically adapt their behavior to the conditions they encounter and to make decisions based on a set of inbuilt rules and criteria, without specific on-the-spot instruction from the user. Agents may possess this feature of autonomy to a greater or lesser degree, depending on their sophistication. The capacity for autonomous behavior may extend to taking the initiative, for example providing the user with information not specifically requested but likely to be of interest. Agents may also communicate with one another and with other programs or people to obtain information or enlist help. Some are also capable of traveling between host computers (mobile agents).

In the area of Internet information searching, intelligent agents use their autonomy to add another dimension to traditional search facilities. For instance, they may decide how and where to search for a required piece of information, dynamically adapting their actions in response to the network environment as the search is carried out.

Access

An agent can be run on a client (the user's machine) or on a Web server (though mobile agents are not confined to a single location and may travel from client to server). There is a great deal of client-based agent software available on the Web for a range of platforms. Some are free, but many agent packages are commercial products available for purchase. Server-based agents (for example, Excite Product Finder) can be accessed via their URLs. Some of these online agents may require users to go through a registration process which gives them a reusable login and password.

Coverage

Agent software is used in a variety of contexts such as system administration, information searching on the Internet, current awareness services, online shopping, and so on. Some of the specific tasks which agents can be used for include:

- to enrich the user's net browsing by suggesting additional hyperlinks, based on previous user behavior;

- to give added value to search engine searches;

- to run searches on multiple databases, filter and assemble the results in an intelligent way;

- to find the best price for a given product from online markets;

- to engage in transactions and negotiations on behalf of the user;

- to monitor databases on the WWW and provide a regular updating service;

- to monitor Web site changes;

- to compile a daily personalized newspaper;

- to visit sites nominated by the user and download either the entire site or selected pages for offline viewing;

- to discover other people with common interests;

- to check and prioritize email, make decisions based on content and act on them.

Using

Some intelligent agents have inbuilt sets of rules and criteria already in place, or their task is a circumscribed one. These require little or no configuration. Others need to be 'trained'. That is, they can be provided with sets of rules by the user. This may be a more time-consuming process, but in the end, will give a product tailor-made to individual requirements.

EXAMPLES

BotSpot **http://www.botspot.com** gives many examples of bots and agents.

Autonomy at **http://www.autonomy.com** has developed a suite of products using agent technology to generate personalized, organized content from large bodies of unstructured online information. The Autonomy software focuses on concepts occurring in text, taking into account their frequency and context, and adapts over time to improve on its recognition of the same concepts. The technology is used in products for new media publishing and knowledge management such as Content Infrastructure, Knowledge Server, Knowledge Update and Portal-in-a-Box.

CareerSite **http://www.careersite.com** is an example of the practical application of agent technology. It uses confidential candidate profiles and concept-based searches to link employers with job seekers.

In common with a number of other portal services, Excite Live **http://live.excite.com** provides personalized entry to its information service. On registering, the user is asked to fill in a form and thereafter at login, gets a personalized version of Excite's information service. The personal profile is progressively added to by NewsTracker which learns more about the user's favorite topics as users respond to and rate the articles it returns.

Another example of agent technology on the Excite site is Excite Shopping (**http://www.jango.com**) employing Jango agent software which was designed specifically for shopping on the net.

eWatch at **http://www.ewatch.com** is an example of an agent-based alerting service available through subscription. It monitors mailing lists, newsgroups, forums and Web sites for information on insider trading, stock manipulation, rumors and anti-corporate activism. The MediaXpress service from Wavo Corporation at **http://go.to/mediaxpress** delivers information from leading media and information providers in real time using push technology.

Finding more information

A wide range of agent resources is available from the UMBC AgentWeb Web site.

An Agent Development Kit (ADK) is available from Tryllian via their Web site at **http://www.tryllian.com/**

1.9 METADATA

Organizing the Web

The use of metadata to add 'cataloguing' information to Web resources is one potential way of improving the organization of Web resources and allowing the development of more sophisticated search tools.

Metadata

Metadata is simply 'information about information'. A library catalogue record or publishing details contained at the start of a book are examples of metadata – information that describes information. The lack of metadata on the Web is currently a great impediment to effective searching. It is almost impossible to search for the author of a Web page and restricting searches by date is also problematic – what exactly is the 'date' of a Web page? When it was first written or last updated? Even if date information is added to a Web page, there are no rules that govern the format of a date – for example is 03/04/00 the 3rd of April or the 4th of March?

Metadata is written into the code of a Web page, so that it is not displayed on the page, but can be indexed by search tools. Web pages are written in the HTML language which uses 'tags' to define parts of a page. 'Meta-tags' are placed in an unseen part of the Web page called the HEAD (what appears in the browser window is what is written in the BODY of a page). The most commonly used meta-tags are the keyword and description tags. The information contained in the description tag is often what is displayed in results listings in search engines. There are formalized schemes being developed to define which meta-tags should be used – the Dublin Core scheme defines 15 different metadata elements, including title, creator, publisher and resource type.

Unfortunately, the use of metadata is open to abuse by Web authors who want to get their sites listed higher in search engines – they repeat keywords over and over again, an activity known as keyword or index spamming. If this is detected by a search engine, the site will be penalized by being removed from the index.

EXAMPLE

This is an example of metadata (Dublin Core scheme):

```
<meta name="DC.Publisher" content="Netskills, University of
Newcastle, UK">
<meta name="DC.Date" content="2000-02-10">
<meta name="DC.Identifier"
content="http://www.netskills.ac.uk/">
<meta name="DC.Format" content="text/html - 6,975 bytes">
<meta name="DC.Type" content="Text">
```

Further information

Dublin Core Metadata Initiative **http://purl.org/DC/**

W3C Metadata and Resource Description **http://www.w3.org/Metadata/**

Desire Project: Information Toolkits **http://www.desire.org/toolkit/**

2

SPECIALIST SEARCH TOOLS

In addition to the general Web searching facilities, there are specialist search tools which address particular search requirements or specific categories of Internet information. The topics dealt with here include:

- directory services
- searching for people, organizations and software
- databases
- local services
- keeping current

2.1 DIRECTORY SERVICES

Online directory services can be divided into two groups, White Pages and Yellow Pages. White Pages provide a means of searching for people and computers on the Internet. Yellow Pages provide for searching for businesses. While there is no comprehensive stand-alone global directory, some of the Web directories mentioned in Section 2.2 boast impressive tallies of names. This section covers a selection of tools commonly used for providing Internet directory services. Some of the tools such as CSO and Whois are used mainly for local directories, while others such as X.500 and LDAP can be used globally. Though the net cast by these tools collectively catches the contact details of millions of people, there are still many people covered only by local directories which use tools other than those listed here.

See also Section 2.2 for general guidelines on the topic.

Directory services tools covered here:

- CSO
- LDAP
- X.500
- Whois
- Whois++

2.1.1 CSO

CSO is an abbreviation of CCSO which stands for Computing and Communications Services Office at the University of Illinois, Urbana-Champaign where it was developed. Many universities use CSO to make student and staff information (for example, phone numbers, email addresses) available online. While the data collected may vary from one organization to another, a CSO directory can usually be searched by name, email address, department, and so on.

Access

CSO directories are made available via a server (Phonebook Server). The server is accessed with a ph client, either stand-alone (for example, WinPH for Windows), or built into a WWW gateway. Also the mail program Eudora includes a ph client. The client is configured by the user to access a specific CSO server to search for information.

CSO is normally used to provide the directory of a single organization only. It is therefore necessary for the user to know which organization or server to run a search on. For links to services worldwide, see the University of Illinois' Phonebook Gateway page at **http://www.uiuc.edu/cgi-bin/ph/**

2.1.2 LDAP

LDAP (Lightweight Directory Access Protocol) is a protocol for directory services on the Internet. It is an open protocol, enabling any client program using it to access any LDAP-compliant (or X.500) directory server. An example of its implementation is the email address lookup facility in an LDAP-enabled email client program. The user can specify the LDAP directory to use, for instance, their institution's staff directory. Client and server handle the details of information request and delivery.

LDAP has many similarities to X.500 described in Section 2.1.3. Like X.500 it defines a global directory structure, including how the information in a directory is to be organized as well as the protocol for accessing the information. Unlike X.500, it is simpler in concept and more easily implemented and it also supports TCP/IP.

In common with X.500 the LDAP information model is based on the entry, which contains information about some object (for example, a person). Entries may include a mix of information such as text, JPEG photographs, sounds, URLs and PGP keys. Directory entries are arranged in a hierarchical tree-like structure.

Access

LDAP is implemented in many directory services such as those of Netscape, Novell, Microsoft, Sun. LDAP client access is available in programs such as Eudora Pro 4.0, Netscape Communicator, Microsoft Outlook Express 4.0, Lotus cc:Mail. OpenLDAP **http://www.openldap.org/** is an open source implementation of the Lightweight Directory Access Protocol. There is a list of national LDAP servers and other Public Directory Interfaces at **http://www.dante.net/np/pdi.html**

LDAP sources can be accessed via the Web using the LDAP URL format, for example `ldap://ldap.widgets.com/ou=production,o=widgets,c=nl?one` (this query filters down the directory tree to entries in the production department).

Further information:

Information resources on LDAP and related issues: **http://www.terena.nl/task-forces/tf-lsd/lsd-info.html**

Tools and Software for LDAP/Directory based Internet applications: **http://www.terena.nl/task-forces/tf-lsd/lsd-swtools.html**

Innosoft's LDAP World: **http://www3.innosoft.com/ldapworld/index.html**

2.1.3 X.500

X.500 is a standard for distributed directory services. The standard encompasses both the structure of the X.500 database and also the protocol used in querying the database. X.500 can be used for different types of directories. Its most notable implementation is a global White Pages service containing in excess of a million names contributed to by X.500 servers in dozens of countries.

X.500 provides a hierarchical database structure (for example, country/ organization/organizational unit/person). The database consists of entries (one per object) which may describe persons, network resources, organizations, and so on, each with its own set of attributes.

Access

X.500 is based on the client–server model. The user with an X.500 client (known in the X.500 world as a Directory User Agent or DUA) can query an X.500 server (Directory System Agent or DSA). The server maintains the local X.500 database, but it can also communicate with other X.500 servers. If a query cannot be answered locally it may be passed on automatically to other X.500 servers and the response passed back to the user. To the user, it appears that the entire directory is accessible from the local server. As well as queries, X.500 also supports data management functions (addition, modification and deletion of entries).

A list of Public Directory Interfaces to the Nameflow Paradise service (including WWW, gopher, telnet, LDAP server) is made available by DANTE at **http://www.dante.net/np/pdi.html**

Further information

X.500 Directory related information at **http://www.nexor.com/public/ directory.html**

LDAP World at **http://www.innosoft.com/ldapworld/**

LDAP Roadmap and FAQ at **http://www.kingsmountain.com/ldapRoadmap.shtml**

2.1.4 Whois

Whois is both a directory and a protocol. The Whois directory is a searchable database of information about networks, networking organizations, domains and sites and the contacts associated with them. It can be used in the following ways:

● to find information about networks, domains and hosts;

● to locate contact information (people) for networks and domains;

● when registering a domain name, to see if the name is already in use.

The main Whois database is maintained by Network Solutions. An organization that registers a top-level domain name is automatically added to the Whois database.

Access

Whois can be accessed through a local Whois client, through an interactive telnet session, through email or through the Web-based form at **http://www.networksolutions.com/cgi-bin/whois/whois/**

2.1.5 Whois++

Whois++ is a distributed database protocol for networked data collections. It provides consolidated query access to information such as White Pages or Yellow Pages data dispersed across a large number of servers. It was developed to be backward compatible with the earlier Whois protocol, which it extends with options such as the use of multiple languages and character sets, more advanced search expressions, structured data and optional authentication. Structured data of any type can reside under a Whois++ server.

Access

The NSF Whois++ Testbed Project Web site contains extensive reference material relating to Whois++ and Whois++ products such as Digger. Information about the project is available from **http://www.ucdavis.edu/whoisplus/**

Extensive information about the Whois++ protocol can be found at **http://www.networksorcery.com/enp/protocol/whois++.htm**

2.2 SEARCHING FOR PEOPLE, ORGANIZATIONS AND SOFTWARE

If you plot a five-year graph of the estimated number of people using the Internet, what you will see is a soaring curve steadily reaching more and more of the world's population. Currently there are tens of millions of Internet users which, by any standards, makes the Internet an impressive people resource. Here, almost certainly, there will be people who share your interests, no matter how specialized, esoteric or eccentric. Additionally, the Internet and the many networks embraced by it provide an excellent medium for bringing like-minded people together and enabling them to exchange information and opinions easily.

In another quite different way, networks facilitate communication between people. They may be able to help you locate address information in order to make contact with a specific person. The sections below look at the many sources to consult for information on email addresses and other contact details.

2.2.1 Locating people with common interests

Computer networks offer not only great technical and information resources, they also provide a uniquely effective vehicle for making contact with people who share common interests. They are effective because they provide a fast and efficient means of transmission, and also because they carry tens of thousands of ongoing discussion lists and newsgroups. These give groups of people with a common interest the opportunity for easy exchange of ideas and news on their subject of interest, and may also generate further one-to-one dialogues between like-minded individuals. Networks facilitate the existence of virtual communities united by common interests, irrespective of location, institutional rank, or even social skills. To find others who share your interest in a particular subject, the most useful starting point is to identify mailing lists (discussion lists) or newsgroups which cover the topic. Use one of the services which offer searching by topic such as the following:

- Liszt: **http://www.liszt.com** Large directory of mailing lists and Usenet news-groups. Weekly updating of the database;
- Tile.Net: **http://tile.net** Reference source for finding discussion lists and newsgroups.

Mailing lists

- CataList: the catalogue of LISTSERV lists at **http://www.lsoft.com/lists/listref.html** is a large constantly maintained catalogue of LISTSERV lists offering searching for mailing lists of interest, and browsing of public LISTSERV lists;
- Stephanie daSilva's Publicly Accessible Mailing Lists at **http://paml.alastra.com** is a searchable list of mailing lists available primarily through the Internet, Usenet and the World Wide Web;
- Search the List of Lists at **http://catalog.com/vivian/interest-group-search.html**. The List of Lists was the pioneer 'master list' of email discussion groups;

- JISCmail at **http://www.jiscmail.ac.uk** is a UK-based mailing list service which administers a large number of lists primarily for the UK academic and research community. Membership of public lists is open to anyone. Use its search facility (linked from the home page) to search for lists on serious academic or research topics.

Newsgroups

Deja.com: **http://www.deja.com** offers keyword searching for newsgroups and also searching for newsgroup articles.

2.2.2 Finding contact details for people

On the Internet it is possible to locate email addresses, postal addresses, telephone numbers and fax numbers using searchable online directory services. What is not possible is to give any guarantees about what might or might not be able to be found. There is no universal directory of Internet users, nor even comprehensive coverage of names within any one country. And coverage is certainly unequal from country to country and from discipline to discipline. On the plus side, the existing directories contain millions of names and corresponding contact details. As well as the White Pages and Yellow Pages services, there are specialized directories such as directories of professional groups, databases of subscribers to mailing lists, campus and organizational directories, and a directory of people who have posted articles to Usenet newsgroups. Almost universally, these services are available via the World Wide Web.

The information contained in the directories on the Internet may be sourced from commercial directory publishers who use phone books and public records to obtain data. Alternatively, it may be generated by a robot which collects data from Web sites. Email addresses may be extracted from Usenet postings, submitted by Internet Service Providers (ISPs), and/or a range of manually collected sources such as organizational staff listings, or self-submitted details from users. Internet directory services may use a variety of technologies. The service may rely on a database held in a single location and interrogated from a single point using some sort of index searcher, or it may use a distributed database accessed through a common protocol such as LDAP, Whois, or X.500. Information on popular tools for building and accessing directory services can be found under Directory Services.

Some of the leading people-finding services are now to be found under the umbrella of portal services, e.g:

- **The Ultimate Directory**: http://www.infospace.com Offers searching for email addresses, telephone and fax numbers, businesses, company Web sites, and other material. Yellow Pages offers multiple search options for US companies, plus links to directories and information for a selection of other countries. White Pages offers searching to locate residential phone numbers and email addresses of individuals.

- **Lycos Networld**: http://www.whowhere.lycos.com Offers the WhoWhere People Finder in which you can search for email addresses, search for phone and postal addresses and Yellow Page listing for the USA. For finding phone numbers for other countries, there are links to telephone and business directories by country. Also on this site is a Web site search, as well as a number of specialist searches mainly oriented to US users.

There are also major sites dedicated exclusively to directory services:

- Bigfoot: **http://www.bigfoot.com** Provides searching of email addresses, the Web and US Yellow Pages.

- WED: **http://worldemail.com** Provides multilingual service (English, Dutch, French, German, Italian and Spanish) with a database of over 18 million email addresses and 140,000 business and phone addresses worldwide. It is a combined Personal Directory, Phone and Fax Directory, Business Directory, Yellow Pages, White Pages, Zip Code Directory, Email Directory, Homepage Directory all in one.

Searching phone numbers is generally patchy, nevertheless there are a number of searchable national telephone directory services available on the Internet. In addition to the umbrella services mentioned above, international telephone directories can be accessed from the following sites:

- The Global Yellow Pages: **http://www.globalyp.com/world.htm** Provides links to national residential telephone and business directories.

- Euroinfo: **http://www.infobel.be/inter/world.asp** Offers searching of phone, fax and email directories by country, searching of business directories.

2.2.3 Finding email addresses

One of the most common requirements for network users wanting to correspond with others is for information on email addresses. Here are some suggestions for finding the email address of a would-be correspondent:

1 Ask them! (Use the phone if necessary.)

2 Ask them to email you first, then use your email program's 'Reply' function. This generates their email address in the 'To:' field of the message. Make a note of it for future reference, or better still, get your email program to make a note of it for you. Most email programs will have such a facility, entitled 'Nicknames', 'Aliases', or something similar.

3 Search an online directory service. Here are some which have substantial databases of names, though note that not all information in directories may be 100 per cent current:

   - Yahoo! People Search: **http://people.yahoo.com** Offers a simple and an advanced email search.
   - Internet Address Finder: **http://www.iaf.net** Offers searching by name in its database of over 6 million email addresses. Versions in Dutch, French, German, Italian and Portuguese.
   - LDAP (see Section 2.1.2) is a standard for directory services enabling a user with an LDAP client to access any LDAP or X.500 server. LDAP is widely implemented, being embedded in all popular Web browsers and email clients.
   - Directory services X.500 (see Section 2.1.3) is the more complex forerunner of LDAP enabling global search of distributed X.500 directories or searches of specific X.500 directories. See the list of public directory interfaces at **www.dante.net/np/pdi.html**

4 Databases of mailing list subscribers and Usenet news contributors are another useful source for email addresses, particularly if your correspondent is an Internet enthusiast and likely to participate in online discussions. These are ones to try:

   - Remarq/Critical Path: **http://www.remarq.com** A database listing over 700,000 messages from 38,000 newsgroups. It has a facility to search for the author of a message, as well as searching the messages themselves.
   - Deja.com: **http://www.deja.com/usenet** There are options here to search for the authors of Usenet messages.

5 Organizational directory listings. If your would-be correspondent is at a university or research institute, the institution's staff list may provide the information you need. Institutional Web sites (Web search services may be useful in locating particular ones) will commonly provide a link to a searchable directory listing of personnel. A site that can be used to locate organizational directories is:

   - GALILEI: **http://www.galilei.com.ar/index.html** International directory of universities and similar institutions enabling you to find the Web sites of individual universities anywhere in the world.

6   Professional listings provide another possible source of contact details. Web search services may be useful for locating the Web sites of professional associations.

  – Martindale-Hubbell Lawyer Locator: **http://www.martindale.com/ locator/home.html** Example of a professional database. Searching on a database of 900,000 lawyers and law firms around the world.

2.2.4 Searching for companies and organizations

There are a number of approaches to searching for companies and organizations on the Internet. Many companies and organizations now have their own Web pages, so Web search services are a good starting point. There are also directories and databases not directly indexed by search engines. The following approaches may be useful:

● Type the name of the organization into your Web browser's Location Window and let it conduct a search for the home page.

● Conduct a keyword search of a search engine database (use as many terms as possible, for example organization name, type of organization, product, location).

● Consult business directories in the portal services listed in Section 1.7.

● Use the online email, telephone and fax directories mentioned in Section 2.2.2 above. A number of these provide a search facility for US businesses, but also give links to business directories for other countries.

● Consult Global Business Centre at **http://www.glreach.com/gbc/index.php3** This is a multiple language Web site with links to business and directory information by country.

● Consult YellowWeb Europe at **http://www.yweb.com/index2.html** This is a European Web guide designed to provide easy multilingual access to European service listings.

2.2.5 Finding and retrieving software

Computer networks are great treasure troves of computer software. Public archives on the Internet and other networks contain millions of public domain and shareware software packages which are easily accessed and downloaded. An ethos of free exchange and sharing, a climate of experimentation and development, and a potent concentration of computing talent have generated these enormous quantities of good working software available at little or no cost, with developers enjoying the benefits of network distribution, testing and feedback. Much of the software is in the public domain and free; there is also a good deal of shareware. Shareware requires a modest payment to the author, but even here there is usually a free trial period allowed.

The Internet also provides access to software from commercial software companies such as Microsoft, Adobe and others. Some is available at no cost, such as Netscape Communicator, Microsoft Internet Explorer or Adobe Acrobat Reader. Commercial software may be purchased via the Internet using a credit card, with security mechanisms such as Secure Sockets Layer (SSL) used to safeguard the data transmitted between browser and server. For buyers who are uneasy about sending their encrypted credit card details over the Internet, the vendors usually provide alternative routes for payment. For more information on security see Chapter 5.

Knowing that there is a lot of software available is cheering, but browsing through cryptically signposted ftp archives is a very frustrating exercise. For effective use of ftp resources, it's advisable to be aware of a few useful tools and services. Some suggestions follow.

Make use of WWW software directories

When you come to look for a software package, some of the large well-organized WWW software directories are a useful starting point (see 'Selected WWW software directories' below). They classify each item within a broad category making it possible to browse purposefully, whether or not you can put a name to the software you need. They also offer searching. If you know what you want the software to do, then you should be able to search for it. For instance, you could search for a paint program using the search term 'paint', or an ftp client with the search term 'ftp'. And you would be able to specify the operating system for which it is required.

Note: While most reputable ftp sites will check the software that they archive to ensure that it does not harbor viruses, you should still ensure that you are running an up-to-date virus checker on your computer.

Familiarize yourself with ftp

Ftp (File Transfer Protocol) is used in downloading files from ftp archives, or uploading files to your own directory on a remote server. Basically, ftp is just an agreed set of commands used between ftp clients and servers.

Anonymous ftp

There is a very useful enhancement of ftp called anonymous ftp. This is a convention which effectively provides open access to software in public ftp archives. There are two main routes for using anonymous ftp:

- **ftp connection using an ftp client** When prompted for a login, type in anonymous, then give your email address as the password. If you are transferring binary files (most files except for READMEs and files with filename extensions such as .txt, .ascii, .hqx, .ps, .uue), you need to set the transfer mode as binary before starting the transfer. Use the client's Help facility for information on commands.

- **ftp using a Web browser** Any file in a public ftp archive can be accessed via the Web as long as you have the host name (the domain name) of the ftp server and the path. The browser takes care of the login and password conventions and also sorts out the mode of transfer (text or binary). You only need to remember to specify ftp (the protocol to be used) as the first part of the URL, for example ftp://isis.cshl.org/pub/wusage/wusage3.2.tar.z

Archive searching services are useful when you know what you want

There are a number of programs that search through Internet file archives, generate an index, and provide a search facility on the index. An example is:

- Lycos Pro Search: **http://ftpsearch.lycos.com**

There are also some national services providing searching of ftp servers in one country only, for example:

- NoseyParker: **http://sunsite.uakom.sk/Parker/search.html**, a Czech search engine.

Use an ftp site near to you

Commonly, ftp sites which are heavily used or which have a widely dispersed user group will be mirrored. This means that the whole structure and contents of the archive will be duplicated elsewhere. This distributes the load on the server, and makes retrieving files more efficient for users. Regular automated updating ensures that the mirror site is in step with the original collection. (See the UK Mirror Service at **http://www.mirror.ac.uk**)

Where there is a choice of sites offering the same software, it's usually a good idea to retrieve from the nearest one. It's faster for you and good for the network environment. For instance, if you are in Europe, give preference to a European site over an American one.

Learn how to handle compressed files and other formats

If you retrieve files from ftp archives, you will soon come across compressed and archived file formats. Compressing files, or packaging up multiple files into a single archive file is common practice. Files take up less storage space and are quicker and easier to transfer. To compress a file requires compression software. When you retrieve such a file, normally you will need to have complementary decompression software to restore the file to its original form. The same principle applies with archived files and also with binary files which have been converted to text (encoded).

When you retrieve a file which has undergone one of these processes, note the file extension because this gives a clue to the software needed to restore the file to its original form. See the tables in Appendix A for additional detail.

Selected WWW software directories

TUCOWS: **http://www.tucows.com**
TUCOWS is a popular source for Internet software for Windows and Macintosh platforms, and also Linux, Java and PDAs. Within each platform, programs are grouped under categories such as Audio, Browsers, Communications, Connectivity, Email, HTML Tools, Multimedia, Security, etc., and a search facility is available. For fast downloads, the collection is mirrored at many sites in many countries. Each program gets a brief standard entry including access details and a rating based on its functioning, design and usefulness.

Shareware.com: **http://www.shareware.com**
Shareware.com from CNet offers a search of a number of existing Internet software archives containing 250,000 freeware and shareware (software that you can try before you buy) files. It includes software for PC, Mac, Unix, Amiga and

Atari. You can select your operating system then run a keyword search to generate a list of entries on relevant software. You can also search in specific shareware archives. Entries include size and date information on the package, and for some packages, useful descriptions as well. The site includes a list of 'Top Picks' for PC and Mac.

Download.com: **http://download.cnet.com**
Download.com from CNet offers access to more than 20,000 Windows, Macintosh, DOS, Linux, Palm OS, Windows CE and BeOS freeware, shareware and demo software programs that are available for download over the Internet. The programs are categorized under headings such as Business & Finance, Desktop Enhancements, Development Tools, Drivers, Home & Education, Games, Internet, Multimedia & Design and Utilities, and there is also a search facility. Informative descriptive entries on each program offer links to reviews and download sites.

Filemine: **http://www.filemine.com**
Filemine offers an integrated index to programs on archive sites and mirror sites around the world. It includes shareware for PC, Mac, Amiga, Unix, Atari. Programs are grouped in categories such as Business, Internet, Multimedia, Desktop Tools, Home & Leisure, and then within a subcategory. Most are given a brief entry with evaluation rating based on ease of use, interface, documentation and performance. Some specially selected programs (Jewels) get lengthy descriptions.

ZDNet Software Library: **http://www.zdnet.com/downloads/**
This library classifies its contents by category, and provides an informative descriptive entry on each with an evaluation. ZDNet's library lists thousands of software packages in categories such as Games, Internet, Home and Education, and so on. You can browse the archive or do a keyword search.

Jumbo!: **http://www.jumbo.com**
Jumbo groups software packages under headings such as Internet, Multimedia, at the top level. Entries on each item include at least a definition, file size and date. It's possible to upload programs as well as download them.

Nerd's Heaven: **http://boole.stanford.edu/nerdsheaven.html**
This is not a software directory but a list of sites relevant to the task of obtaining software. It includes links to many more software directories than are mentioned here, and also links to notable archive sites for specific categories of software such as Internet, operating systems, mathematical software, software for Windows and other platforms.

2.3 DATABASES

Some of the most valuable resources accessible via the Internet are the many specialist databases used as everyday working tools by librarians, scientists and other professionals. For instance online bibliographic databases are the stock-in-trade of librarians, and scientific datasets figure prominently in many scientific disciplines. Many, though not all, online databases are subscription or fee-based and are accessed with a user-id and password. To locate online databases for a given subject, use services such as:

- Direct Search: **http://gwis2.circ.gwu.edu/~gprice/direct.htm** links directly to the search interfaces of resources that are not easily searchable from search engines;

- InvisibleWeb at **http://www.invisibleweb.com** is a database-based searching facility.

- Lycos Searchable Databases at **http://dir.lycos.com/Reference/ Searchable_Databases** provide access to a range of searchable databases.

Examples of online databases include:

- UnCover Web: **http://www.ingenta.com**, a periodicals database;

- Physics E-print archive: **http://babbage.sissa.it**, which provides pre-prints of physics journal articles.

2.4 LOCAL SERVICES

Geographically specialized search engines and directories are very useful in searching for local, regional or national information. The USA is generally well provided for by the well-known general services, though many of these provide additional country-specific search services, e.g. AltaVista, Lycos, Yahoo! and Excite. Search engines which specialize in European resources are:

- Euroferret **http://www.euroferret.com/**
- EuroSeek **http://www.euroseek.com**

Classified directories include:

- ukdirectory **http://www.ukdirectory.com**

Subject listings of sites

- Index of Swedish WWW Pages **http://www.sunet.se/**

2.5 KEEPING CURRENT

The Internet is a great source for maintaining professional awareness and keeping current with general news about events at home and abroad. As well as the obvious sources of online newspaper and magazines, there are many news alerting services, some of which can be customized to fit your interests. Many of the general portal services include current news and, if you register with them, may offer a personalized news service with selections tailored to interest. Push technology can be used to deliver news feeds, sending the information to the user's client as it becomes available.

Another technology used in keeping current is the intelligent agent (see Section 1.8.2) or bot. This is a program which may be installed on the user's machine and instructed on what to search for and how often. The use of intelligent agents to generate personalized news on a regular basis means that users can exercise control over the information that comes to them, rather than be the passive recipients of a predetermined selection of news from a remote server. The agent may make its own decisions on where to go to find the required information.

Many Web information services include a What's New page. When useful sites and subject resources are already known, a regular check on their What's New pages using agent software or a service like Mind-It is a useful means of keeping current in a subject area. Some relevant sources are described below.

Current events

- BotSpot: **http://bots.internet.com** The latest and greatest news bots.
- EntryPoint: **http://www.entrypoint.com** Example of the use of push technology to get personalized news and information via 'channels' covering news, companies, industries, weather, sports and lifestyles. The locally installed

EntryPoint software goes into action when the computer is not in use – news is displayed in the screensaver.

- GO Network: **http://www.go.com** Example of a portal service providing a personalized opening page with the selection of news stories and other information tailored to preferences specified on registration.

- Lycos: **http://www.lycos.com** Provides a News section with up to the minute stories tailored to user's domain. Offered in Germany, Belgium, Switzerland, Spain, France, Italy, Netherlands, Denmark, Sweden, UK, USA, Japan.

New Internet resources

- Yahoo! What's New at **http://dir.yahoo.com/new/** provides links to new entries of interest in the Yahoo! database.

- whatsnew.com at **http://www.whatsnew.com** lists new Web sites relating to travel, entertainment news and tickets.

- Classroom Connect at **http://listserv.classroom.com/archives/** announces Internet resources, especially those of interest to the education community. Current and archived postings can be read and searched at this Web site. It is also available via email and Usenet newsgroups.

- Scout Report at **http://wwwscout.cs.wisc.edu/report/sr/current/** gives new and newly discovered Internet resources and network tools of interest to researchers and educators.

- Internet Resources Newsletter is at **http://www.hw.ac.uk/libWWW/irn/irn.html**

Descriptive listing of new sites (not searchable):

- Researchbuzz News at **http://www.researchbuzz.com/news/** lists new resources of interest to the researcher. Available by email as well.

Changed Internet resources

Mind-it at **http://www.netmind.com/html/users.html** lets you track changes to specified Web pages, or sections within a page, or keywords of interest, notifying you by email when there are changes.

3

COMMUNICATION AND SHARING INFORMATION

This chapter describes the various tools and technologies which can be used to communicate on the Internet. Some tools (e.g email) are used for one-to-one communication; others permit one-to-many or many-to-many communication (e.g newsgroups).

Asynchronous communication

Some of these tools do not require simultaneous connection between the message sender and the recipient. For example, when an email is sent it is read at the convenience of the recipient. This is known as 'asynchronous' communication.

Synchronous communication

Other tools involve a 'live' communication between the parties which requires them to be connected at the same time. For example, Internet video or audioconferencing. This is known as 'synchronous' communication. Synchronous communication is employed by a whole swathe of tools which enable the people involved to connect simultaneously and communicate interactively with each other. These real-time communication tools come in a variety of media, ranging from plain text to full-blown multimedia.

Collaboration

Finally, collaboration tools may combine both modes of communication to allow users to colloborate on a piece of work.

This chapter covers the following groups of tools:

- Asynchronous tools
  - Email
  - Mailing lists
  - Usenet News (newsgroups)
  - Web conferencing
- Synchronous tools
  - Chat (IRC)
  - Videoconferencing
  - Audioconferencing/Internet telephony – MBone
  - Streaming
- Collaboration
  - Group collaboration
  - Collaborative functions
  - Software for collaboration
  - File Exchange and Transfer (FTP)

3.1 EMAIL

Electronic mail (usually just referred to as email) is a system for the transmission of messages and files between computers. It enables you to send text messages to other email users conveniently, quickly and cheaply. You use an email program on your computer to access and read email and to send messages. When you send a message it is delivered to your correspondent's mailbox where it waits until they collect it and read it. Email also provides an effective mechanism for the distribution of information to many people simultaneously, for example through the use of mailing lists (see Section 3.2).

Becoming an email user

To use email, you need access to a computer connected to the Internet and you need to register as an email user with your organization or with an Internet Service Provider. You will also need to install an email program on your computer, such as Microsoft Outlook, Eudora or Pegasus. Alternatively, you can register for a Web-based email account such as Hotmail (**http://www.hotmail.com**) which is free and only requires a Web browser.

Finally, you will also be given an email address which will probably take the form mailname@host (for example, john.allan@sons.org.uk). This is an Internet email address, where 'host' is the computer's Internet address. The mailname might be some form of your own name or your computer user-id. No one else whose mail is on the same host computer will have the same mailname. It is unique for that host, just as that host's address is unique on the Internet.

Transmission of files

Email also allows for the fast and easy transmission of any sort of document or computer file (for example, Word documents, spreadsheets or anything else).

Using modern email packages, sending files by email is a matter of selecting the menu option to attach a document to a mail message. The email program normally takes care of the process of converting the document to plain-text (ASCII) format, a necessary preliminary to sending documents via Internet email because not all mail servers through which the mail might go can handle binary formats. So, word-processed documents, spreadsheets, images and other binary files, need to be converted to plain text before sending. There are a number of ways in which this can be achieved as described below.

MIME

The MIME (Multipurpose Internet Mail Extensions) standard originated because of the need to send non-ASCII documents through Internet email which, at the time, could not handle binary files. MIME is incorporated into much email software. With a MIME-compliant mailer, information is added to the header of the message specifying the type of content included in the message and also specifying how the content is encoded. Various types of content can be specified, including binary data, images, audio and video files.

For example, if the message is a text file in the Croatian language using the ISO-8859-2 character set, the mailer inserts a line in the header of the message:

```
Content-type: text/plain; charset=iso-8859-2
```

where iso-8859-2 is a registered MIME name for a character set.

Content-Type Defaults are

```
Content-type: text/plain; charset=us-ascii
```

If a GIF file is included, the mailer inserts a line like this in the header of the message:

```
Content-Type: Image/Gif
```

MIME usually uses Base64 for encoding binary files. This may be indicated in the header with a line like this:

```
Content-Transfer-Encoding: base64
```

Quoted Printable is another encoding technique most appropriate for ASCII files with a small section of non-ASCII characters. If the receiving mailer is MIME-compliant, it will correctly interpret the lines in the header and decode and display or save the file appropriately.

Uuencode

Uuencode is a method of encoding binary files to plain text which originated on Unix systems, though software for other platforms is also available. Uuencode (and Uudecode) is incorporated into a number of mail packages. Exchanges between different systems using uuencode may not be entirely reliable as it has not been standardized.

BinHex

BinHex originated with Apple Macs and is primarily and seamlessly handled by many Mac applications, and also many PC applications such as Microsoft Internet Explorer and Netscape Navigator.

Dedicated conversion software is available for a number of platforms. When a message with an attached encoded document is received, the recipient's email program steps in, taking care of decoding, saving, and so on. Commonly, the message will include an icon representing the file. From there the user can select and display the file with a simple mouse click. If the email program does not have the required decoding facility it will probably save the file to some default directory leaving the user to locate and open the appropriate decoding application. This is cumbersome at the best of times, but doubly so if this is all an unfamiliar process. Therefore, if you send files to people you should first establish that their mail program can handle the format you intend to use. A simple question like 'Is your mail program MIME-compliant?' can avoid headaches.

Size of files and compression

The same considerations apply to files which are compressed as well as encoded. Some mail systems can handle large transmissions but it is not uncommon for large files or messages (e.g. above 500K) sent by email to be broken down into smaller chunks. While sophisticated mail programs may handle reconstituting these adequately, a safer option for large files is to reduce the size by first compressing them, or to make them available through ftp rather than email. (More information about ftp can be found in Section 3.6.)

Transmission of viruses

Exchanging files by email is one of the great conveniences of the Internet. However it is not without its downside, specifically, the transmission of viruses, which may reside in seemingly innocuous sources such as word-processed files. Word macro viruses can be transmitted by innocent parties exchanging files by email. The Melissa virus extended the insidious effects of the macro virus genre by propagating itself through further multiple email transmissions of an infected document, using the Microsoft Outlook address book to generate a list of recipients. Macro viruses will reproduce only if the automatic execution of macros is enabled in the targeted application, so the precaution is to disable macro execution by default.

Further online resources about computer viruses are available from **http://www.cert.org/other_sources/viruses.html**

More information about the Melissa virus is available from **http://www.cert.org/advisories/CA-1999-04.html**

Finding email addresses

Finding email addresses is not always straightforward as there is no one comprehensive directory. See Section 2.2.3 for guidance.

3.2 MAILING LISTS

Mailing lists enable people with a common interest to meet (virtually), exchange views, circulate news and announcements, make documents available to each other and pool their expertise to solve common problems. The discussion on a mailing list normally focuses on a single subject, though this subject may be a fairly broad one, encompassing many subtopics.

How do mailing lists work?

The facility for sending one message to multiple recipients is common to all email programs. Multiple email addresses can be grouped under one collective name, often referred to as an alias by the email program. This means that you can in fact have a sort of home-made mailing list from your local mail program, adding and removing addresses from the alias manually.

Dedicated mailing list manager software running on a server offers the greatest functionality and capability for large-scale management of mailing lists. Most lists are managed by one or other of several highly developed Mailing List Managers (MLMs), such as LISTSERV, Majordomo, Listproc and Mailbase. Mailing list manager software may provide some or all of the following functions:

- automated processing of subscriptions,
- distribution of messages,
- making available files associated with the list such as the monthly archives of messages,
- searching and indexing of message archives via the Web.

Each mailing list will have a person responsible for the list's operation. This is the list owner. The list owner will see that the list runs smoothly, provide any necessary information files, answer questions from members, and so on. Some lists are open to anyone. Others are closed, in which case the list owner will probably invite selected individuals to join the list and add them manually.

Setting up a mailing list

There are thousands of mailing lists on a vast variety of topics. Refer to Section 2.2.1 for sources to search for mailing lists on a specific topic.

If you cannot find a list on the topic of your interest, you might look at setting up a list yourself. See the List Owner's Manual for LISTSERV at **http://www.lsoft.com/ manuals/ownerindex.html** for guidelines on running a LISTSERV list.

Joining a mailing list

Joining a mailing list is very simple. You send an email message containing a 'subscribe' or a 'join' command to the administrative address of the list. This usually looks something like this:

```
subscribe <listname> <YourFirstName> <YourLastName>
```

Substitute as appropriate between the angle brackets. Usually, you will then receive a message informing you that you are now subscribed to the list.

It is important to remember that the 'subscribe' message, and other administrative messages as well, should go to the administrative address, not to the list itself. With an automated mailing list, administrative messages are processed automatically by the MLM. If you send such messages to the list itself, they will normally be distributed to every subscriber to the list, which besides generating a certain amount of irritation, wastes everyone's time including your own, as your message won't have achieved the intended objective.

Some mailing lists may have a moderator who weeds out unsuitable messages (such as 'subscribe') before they are distributed to the list, or possibly a smart MLM will reject such messages, but this cannot be assumed.

Here are some examples of administrative addresses:

```
LISTSERV@TERENA.NL

mailbase@mailbase.ac.uk
```

and an example of a list address:

```
child-health@mailbase.ac.uk
```

Commands

Mailing list managers respond to commands in email messages. Commonly, they will handle commands to:

- subscribe to a list,
- leave a list,
- receive a list in digest format,
- suspend mail temporarily,
- obtain a list of subscribers,
- obtain a list of archive files,
- search and retrieve archive files.

Consult the MLM's Help file (send an email to the administrative address with the text help) for information on their commands or see a comparative listing of MLM commands by James Milles of Saint Louis University Law Library available at numerous mirror sites, e.g.: **http://cn.net.au/mailser.html**

Handling mailing list correspondence

Some lists are very active and generate a lot of messages each day. With others weeks may go by without any traffic. If you belong to a mailing list you need to learn to cope with the mail it generates. When there is a lot of incoming mail, you need to be discriminating about the email you read and the email you retain. The initial filtering of messages can be done by scanning the Subject field of messages and deleting those you recognize as not relevant to you. If your mail program has a filtering capability, you can configure it to sort (and delete) nominated categories of incoming mail. Whichever filtering process you use, you'll need to act decisively on the messages that remain. Decide which messages should be discarded, which acted upon, and which retained for reference, then follow up accordingly. Set up a logical filing system for retained messages. Later when you need the information, it's useful to be able to refer to all the correspondence on one particular subject.

Make use of the facilities which the mailing list provides. For instance you may opt for a daily digest of messages (all the messages put together in one message), or suspend the list while you are on holiday. If the mailing list provides a browsable archive of messages, you can always refer to that to see what you have missed. In fact, with some busy mailing lists, regular scanning of the message archive for items of interest may be preferable to subscribing.

3.2.1 LISTSERV

LISTSERV, from L-Soft International, is a system for the creation, management and control of electronic mailing lists. It is the most widely deployed mailing list manager package on the Internet and millions of LISTSERV list messages are sent every day. For large-scale distribution of messages, L-Soft also offers the LSMTP mail delivery server.

LISTSERV lists are maintained by LISTSERV servers (listservers). For each list that it maintains, a listserver will manage the subscriber list, distribute list messages, make associated documents available, log mail traffic, archive messages and also carry out database searches of archives and files in response to email commands.

Access

There are versions of LISTSERV for VM, VMS, Unix (13 brands), and Windows 95/98/NT. A free version, LISTSERV Lite, is available for small-scale non-profit mailing list management (up to 10 mailing lists).

Anyone with access to email can join a public LISTSERV list. Simply send a subscribe message to the listserver, for example send to:

```
LISTSERV@LISTSERV.ACSU.BUFFALO.EDU
```

the message

```
SUBSCRIBE NETTRAIN Mary Smith
```

With a public list, anyone can join or leave, send messages, see who is on the list, search the database, and so on. With private lists, you usually need to apply for membership to the list owner, and only people who are subscribed to the list may send messages and access archived postings.

LISTSERV is an email medium par excellence. Messages are sent to LISTSERV mailing lists by email, and all LISTSERV functions are accessed by email command, from straightforward subscribe and unsubscribe commands through to complex database searching functions. Remember that email commands go to the LISTSERV server, for example `LISTSERV@LISTSERV.ACSU.BUFFALO.EDU`, while messages to the list are sent to the list address, for example `NETTRAIN@LISTSERV.ACSU.BUFFALO.EDU`

With the most recent versions of the LISTSERV software, it is also possible to access some of LISTSERV's functions via the World Wide Web, for instance to read message archives and subscribe to the list.

Some LISTSERV lists may also be available via Usenet News through a gateway. Such newsgroups will come under the hierarchy `bit.listserv`. For instance NETTRAIN is available as a newsgroup titled `bit.listserv.nettrain`.

Coverage

A distributed database of information about all publicly accessible LISTSERV lists is automatically generated and maintained. The chances of finding something relevant are probably quite high given that there are currently more than 110,000 public lists. You can search for lists via the Web at the CataList Reference Web site maintained by L-Soft at **http://www.lsoft.com/lists/listref.html**. Here you can get a broad picture of the scale and variety of LISTSERV lists by browsing through the lists of lists. You can also search for LISTSERV lists by topic, get details on each list, browse message archives and even subscribe.

You can of course access all the same information via email. For instance, you can obtain from any LISTSERV server a list of the lists it maintains, by sending it an email containing the word `List`. To obtain a list of LISTSERV lists dealing with a particular topic, you can make a keyword search of the global list of lists:

```
LIST GLOBAL <keyword>
```

Using

LISTSERV offers a great deal of functionality to support the administration of its mailing lists and to give users a range of options covering the way in which they receive list messages, files and information and request database searches. All of these functions can be accessed through email commands which are placed in the body of the message, for example

```
HELP
```

Email commands are addressed to a LISTSERV server and never to an actual list. If your commands relate to a particular list, it is preferable to send email commands to the specific LISTSERV server which manages that list if you know the address. Otherwise, the general LISTSERV address:

```
LISTSERV@LISTSERV.NET
```

may be used and your message will be forwarded to the correct server. This address can also be used for any information requests, such as Help or Info.

When a LISTSERV server receives an email command, it will ignore the 'Subject:' line of the mail header, so your commands must be in the body of the message. Several commands can be sent to LISTSERV in the same mail message, with each command on a separate line. Table 3.1 gives some examples of useful commands.

For a complete list of LISTSERV commands refer to the Listserv Command Reference **http://www.lsoft.com/manuals/1.8d/owner/appenda.html**

Joining lists

When you join a list, LISTSERV adds to its membership database information on your name and email address and assigns you a default set of list options unless

TABLE 3.1 Obtaining information and files

Command	Meaning
`REVIEW <listname> F=MAIL`	Send a list of subscribers. (F is the format requested. Other options include MIME/text, MIME/Appl, UUencode)
`LISTS`	Send a list of lists maintained by the server
`LIST GLOBAL <keyword>`	Send a list of LISTSERV lists (from any server) with this keyword in the description
`INDEX <listname>`	Send a list of archive files for this list
`GET <filename><filetype> <listname>` `  F=MAIL`	Send this archive file

you specify otherwise. The command SET enables you to change the options to suit yourself. There are additional options on most commands.

Obtaining files

Files can be stored at a LISTSERV server and made available for retrieval by users. There are two types of files stored:

- miscellaneous files relevant to the list deposited by the list owner or administrator;
- archives of email distributed to the list.

Database commands

While the traditional medium for searching LISTSERV databases is by email command, database searches can also be conducted via the Web if the list provides a Web interface to its archive. You can see this demonstrated on the CataList Web site at **http://www.lsoft.com/lists/listref.html**

Suppose you wish to subscribe to the NETTRAIN list at UVBM.BUFFALO.CC.EDU. Your full name is Mark P. Waugh. Send the following command to `LISTSERV@UVBM.BUFFALO.CC.EDU`

```
SUBSCRIBE NETTRAIN Mark P. Waugh
```

Suppose you wish to leave the INFO-MAC mailing list (to which you have already subscribed) at the node CEARN. The command:

```
UNSUBSCRIBE INFO-MAC
```

should be sent to the LISTSERV server at CEARN which manages the INFO-MAC list. To leave all the LISTSERV lists you belong to, send the following command to your nearest (or any) LISTSERV:

```
UNSUBSCRIBE * (NETWIDE
```

Suppose you wish to receive a listing of all mailing lists that have the text 'europe' in their name or title. Send the following command to your nearest (or any) LISTSERV server:

```
LIST GLOBAL EUROPE
```

If you want to stop receiving mail from all the lists at CEARN to which you belong, send the following command to the LISTSERV server at CEARN:

```
SET * NOMAIL
```

Suppose you wish to retrieve the file PCPROG ZIP from a filelist, in XXE file format. Send the following command to the LISTSERV server that holds this file:

```
GET PCPROG ZIP F=XXE
```

Finding more information

LISTSERV provides a copious amount of information about itself and its functionality. A standard set of Help files are available upon request from each LISTSERV server. You can obtain a list of these by sending the email command

INFO to a LISTSERV server. To obtain a list of commonly used commands send an email message containing the word:

    HELP

to:

    LISTSERV@LISTSERV.NET

or to any LISTSERV server.

All of L-Soft's manuals for LISTSERV are available on the World Wide Web at the following URL:

http://www.lsoft.com/manuals/index.html

Resources for list owners

CataList Web site at **http://www.lsoft.com/lists/listref.html**. Select Mailing Lists of Interest to List Owners.

3.3 USENET NEWS

Usenet News, also known as News, is a forum for group discussion, providing distribution and archiving of messages posted to topic-based 'newsgroups'. There are some tens of thousands of newsgroups on almost every subject you can think of. The main broad categories for organization of newsgroups are alt, comp, misc, news, rec, sci, soc, talk standing for alternative, computing, miscellaneous, related to the news system itself, recreational, science, social and talk. Within each of these categories there is a hierarchical ranking of subcategories.

Usenet newsgroups are propagated around the world through a system of 'newsfeeds' to News hosts. With over 30,000 newsgroups currently in existence and the sum total of daily postings amounting to hundreds of megabytes, it is not surprising that organizations running News hosts commonly opt for limited newsfeeds comprising just a selection of newsgroups. For the same reason, messages may be stored for days only before they are discarded to make room for fresh newsfeeds.

Access

Newsgroups can be read at thousands of sites around the world. From the user's point of view, one of the major differences between mailing lists and News is that mailing list messages arrive in your mailbox and newsgroup messages wait for you to come to them. Users read messages using a newsreader program. Some Web browsers come with an inbuilt newsreader or you may use a dedicated newsreader program.

The newsreader accesses the local (or remote) News host using the News protocol, enabling you to pull down as many newsgroups and their contents as you desire. If a newsgroup you are interested in is not taken at your site, you can place a request for it with your local Web administrator. If you don't know whether your site has News access, check with your local computer support people. If you don't have access locally to News, there are also publicly accessible newsgroup archives on the Web.

Coverage

Users sending a News message post it to a particular newsgroup. As well as the main categories mentioned above, there are categories based on particular subject areas (for example, bionet, biz, vmsnet), on geographical areas, on organizations or commercial interests. A fee is usually charged for access to commercial newsgroups. There are newsgroups on subjects ranging from education for the disabled to *Star Trek* and from environmental science to politics in the former Soviet Union. The quality of the discussion in newsgroups may be excellent, but this is not guaranteed. Some newsgroups have a moderator who scans the messages for the group and decides which ones are appropriate for distribution.

Newsgroups can provide a useful source of information and help on technical topics, for example software bugs. They commonly offer an associated list of Frequently Asked Questions (FAQ) to avoid saturating the list with repetitions of the same questions. If the FAQ cannot answer a question, users can post it to the newsgroup and an expert somewhere in the world can often supply the answer.

news.answers is a special-purpose newsgroup dedicated to holding the range of FAQ documents from all newsgroups. A searchable archive of all the FAQs from news.answers is available from the Internet FAQ Consortium.

Using a newsreader

Most, if not all, newsreaders provide the same basic functions:

- Subscribing to newsgroups: your newsreading software will make these groups immediately accessible, so that you can read their contents quickly and easily.

- Unsubscribing from newsgroups: removing groups from your easy access list.

- Reading newsgroup postings: your newsreader presents new messages – postings – to you, and keeps track of which postings you have and have not read.

- Threads of discussion: replies to a posting are grouped together with the original posting, so that the reader can follow the messages within a newsgroup which are part of a particular discussion or a topic.

- Posting to newsgroups: you can participate in group discussions; your newsreader knows where to send your posting.

- Responding to a posting: you can send a response to the newsgroup (often called follow-up) or to the author of a posting (often called reply).

Newsreader programs

Web browsers such as Netscape and Internet Explorer include newsreading software. For instance, IE uses Outlook Express to view and post to News. The first step is to download the list of newsgroups. This can be a very large list depending on the News host. When this is done, you can select the newsgroups you wish to subscribe to. Thereafter these will be the ones which will be downloaded by default. With your subscriptions in place, you can now access the articles which are currently held for each of the newsgroups, read them and post articles to them.

No newsreader is required to participate in the News discussions on Deja.com. This service, as well as containing searchable archives of postings from more than 30,000 newsgroups, offers a Web interface to News where you can participate in discussion once you have registered. You need only your Web browser.

3.4 SYNCHRONOUS AND ASYNCHRONOUS COMMUNICATION

The most widespread means of communication on the Internet are well-established tools such as email, mailing lists, newsgroups and web conferencing. These provide a highly flexible and popular means of network communication for interest groups. A feature of their flexibility is that simultaneous connection between message sender and recipients isn't necessary. This type of communication is known as 'asychronous' communication.

The complementary mode of 'synchronous' communication is employed by a variety of tools which enable the people involved to connect simultaneously and communicate interactively with each other. These real-time communication tools range from the exchange of plain text (Internet chat) to full multimedia. Different collaborative tools may employ one or both modes depending on what is required.

This section covers the following topics:

- Web conferencing
- chat
- videoconferencing
- Internet telephony/audioconferencing
- MBone
- Streaming

3.4.1 Web conferencing

The concept of Web conferencing is similar to that of mailing lists and newsgroups. It allows interest groups to exchange information and opinions via the Web, not interactively, but asynchronously. Web conferences may be publicly accessible or limited to a specified group of people, for example a tutor and his or her remote students. There are many software products available which support Web conferencing and allow the creation of virtual learning or discussion environments. Web conferencing is commonly used to support distance learning students.

Web conferencing software typically allows participants to contribute messages, sort messages by author, date or subject, upload files or engage in real-time chat. Its particular strength is that it uses the Web, which provides a cross-platform, low-cost means of hosting an ongoing discussion, potentially available to readers and contributors anywhere on the Internet or intranet.

Like many other Internet systems, Web conferences operate using the client–server model. There is a server which takes care of the administration of the conferences and maintains the files of messages and subscriptions. And there is a client, which is the program the user uses to access the Web conference. This will usually be a regular Web browser such as Netscape or Internet Explorer, though some Web conferencing systems require their own client software.

Whichever it is, the interface to a Web conference is generally very simple and intuitive. It is often also customized to the look and feel of the organization using the system (e.g. use of corporate logos and colors).

Web conferencing in practice

A Web conference may be entered via a login process. This enables the conference server to keep a record of where users have been and a note of their preferences. Once through the initial process, the user will normally see on the Web page a list of the topics in a conference, possibly with an indication of the number of responses within each topic. From there, the reader can select a topic and browse through the messages.

Some systems allow for subscriptions to particular topics so that a user will see a personally customized view of the conference when he or she logs in. Users can then go straight into the discussions which interest them most. The system may also indicate for each topic the number of messages added since the user's last visit.

Web conferencing software

This section gives information about popular Web conferencing software. For an extensive list which points to examples of use, see Woolley, D., *Conferencing Software for the Web*: at **http://thinkofit.com/webconf/**

FirstClass (Collaborative Classroom GOLD)

Firstclass offers advanced messaging, collaboration and event planning groupware. Features include:

- Internet email including address book and message history,
- threaded messages in restricted or open conferences,
- real-time chat,
- work online or offline,
- drag and drop Web publishing.

Access: via Web browser, an Internet mail client or FirstClass client software. Server software is available for Windows NT and Mac OS and client software for Window NT, 95/98 and Mac OS. A free 60-day trial version of the server software is available from **http://www.softarc.com**

WebBoard

An increasingly popular Web conferencing tool which is being used for teaching, providing online technical support and building online communities. It includes:

- threaded message displays,
- possibility to participate in conferences via email,
- IRC and JavaScript chat,
- file attachments,
- message search feature.

Access: via Web browser or email/news client. Server software available for Windows 95/98/NT. A free 30-day trial version of the server software is available from **http://webboard.oreilly.com**

Allaire Forums

A Web conferencing application which works with ColdFusion, Allaire's software for the creation of interactive Web database applications. Forums offers interactive discussion via the Web. Messages are posted to the conference via Web forms, and archives of discussion are viewed with a Web browser.

Features:

- message exchange,
- archiving of messages and threads,
- subscription to threads to receive new messages via email,
- file exchange,
- configurable interface,
- sophisticated security framework.

Access: conference participants only need a Web browser. The server software can be purchased from Allaire. Runs on Windows NT or Windows 95 Web server. Further details of price, availability and system requirements from **http://www.allaire.com**

Ceilidh

Ceilidh is available for free and offers threaded discussions on the WWW with document sharing. Ceilidh uses only HTTP and no other software than a Web browser is required:

- automatic conversion of messages to hypertext,
- threaded list of messages,
- optional email notification of new messages,
- optional file attachments,
- automatic message expiration.

Access: **http://www.lilikoi.com**

3.4.2 Chat

Chat is a system for the interactive exchange of text messages in real time (synchronously). It offers the advantages of real-time communication without the hardware and bandwidth requirements of multimedia tools such as audio- and videoconferencing. Chat conversations may require special client software, but increasingly standard Internet tools such as Web browsers provide the means of access. Users type in a message in a special box on the screen (e.g. part of a Web page) and replies can be seen appearing on the page as other users type.

Chat conversations at their best are spontaneous and lively and hence chat services are widespread on the Internet. In fact there are thousands of chat groups using Web chat services; many of the groups are recreational, but there are also some serious discussions going on. They feature many users from across the world, and a wide variety of subject areas – with chat 'rooms' organized by subject topic in a similar way to Web conferencing or news. While public chat rooms that catch the most attention sometimes contain frivolous or questionable content, it is usually possible to create a private or restricted room, in which a group of invited members can partake in interactive discussions in a controlled environment.

Examples of public chat services include:

- Delphi Forums **http://www.delphi.com**
- Yahoo! Chat **http://chat.yahoo.com**

IRC (Internet Relay Chat)

IRC (Internet Relay Chat) operates on the same principles as public chat servers from the point of view of the user. It, too, is a real-time conversational system which allows two or more users to communicate interactively via typed messages. As a message is typed, it is immediately transmitted and displayed for each person taking part in the conversation. The difference is in the way in which the servers operate: they use a network of servers, relaying the messages between remote users connected to different servers on the network. Users connect to a certain server and can join or create channels (another name for chat rooms); people can join the channel (sometimes by invitation) and carry out discussions. Usually a channel will also have one person (often the person who creates the channel) who controls and manages the room, for example by setting access permissions or removing unwanted users from the channel.

Access

Like many other Internet tools, both public chat systems and IRC are client–server systems. They are hosted on a server, to which users connect using a chat client. There are many dedicated clients available such as ICQ at **http://web.icq.com/**. Public chat systems are often run from a Web server and accessed using a Web browser, simply by going to the relevant Web page. Some chat services are accessed using Java. For these, you will need a Java-capable Web browser such as Netscape Navigator 3.0 or later or Internet Explorer 3.0 or later.

Chat client software may also come as one tool in a package of communication and collaboration facilities, for example Microsoft NetMeeting which also features videoconferencing and application sharing. IRC is often used via a special piece of client software (although again Java within a Web browser is increasingly used). The first thing to do when you start using IRC is to select the IRC server to which you will connect. A list of servers may be included with your client software.

Coverage

IRC servers link together to form networks that cover much of the world. There are many IRC networks including regional and private ones. The three most notable public ones are called EFnet, UnderNet and DALnet, with EFnet being the original and biggest. Public chat systems are run from a worldwide accessible server in the same way as a Web server, and any users on the Internet with the appropriate Web browser (e.g. with Java enabled) can access them.

Topics of discussion on chat are varied. Technical and political discussions are popular, especially concerning current world events. There are many purely recreational discussions going on all the time (see a list of channels on Yahoo!). IRC may be a way to expand your horizons, as people from many countries and cultures are on the system, 24 hours a day. Most conversations are in English, but there are always channels in German, Finnish, Japanese, and occasionally other languages.

Using

Fundamental to the operation of chat is the room or channel: each channel is one conversation. The number of channels is essentially unlimited. Channels have several characteristics in addition to their name. They can be private, invite-only, limited membership, moderated, and so on. If you don't find a channel which suits you, you can create your own. When you start using IRC, you first select a server to connect to, then nominate one or more nicknames which you will use. You then need to join a channel to start chatting. Your presence will be made known to the others on the channel and everything you type will be seen by them. They can then respond to your messages. With a public chat server, you simply visit the Web page and select one of the rooms from the list, or create your own.

Additional flexibility is provided via commands, enabling you, for instance, to run a parallel conversation with a particular user. The commands are available either from your client's menu, or by typing, depending on the interface you are using. All typed IRC commands begin with a slash, for example /HELP for Help, /LIST for a list of available channels. Often special commands can also be typed or selected from a list, for example to indicate emotions or actions rather than simple messages. The user John selecting 'laugh' may result in the chat system displaying "John Laughs!" to all the users.

Chat tools

ICQ

ICQ from Mirabilis is a dedicated chat client. This exclusivity provides additional functionality and a tool well suited for private forums. You can set up your own list of correspondents from whom you will accept chat requests. When they are registered with the service, the program alerts you when they are online. When set up ICQ stays resident in the background until called upon. Chat sessions and other services are managed by the Mirabilis server.

Features include:

- chat with one or more users,
- private sessions,
- launch of third-party applications such as Internet phone applications,
- file transfer and file server facility,
- automatic exchange of URLs,
- paging service,
- saves messages received while user is offline.

Access: the ICQ software must be downloaded from the Mirabilis site at **http://web.icq.com** and installed. Versions available for Windows and Apple Mac.

Finding more information

RFC 1459 Internet Relay Chat Protocol: **http://www.ietf.org/rfc/rfc1459.txt**

Nicolas Pioch: *A Short IRC Primer* at **http://irchelp.org/irchelp/ircprimer.html**

IRC FAQ: Frequently Asked Questions at **http://www.newircusers.com/nfaq.html**

New Internet Chat: **http://www.ichat.com**

3.4.3 Videoconferencing

Videoconferencing allows two or more remote parties to communicate in real time through the use of a live video and audio link.

Videoconferencing can be used in a variety of ways:

● one-to-one, that is, one site with another site;

● one-to-many, that is, a broadcast to many sites, for instance a lecture;

● many-to-many, that is, more than two remote parties take part.

Some applications switch the active video transmission from one location to the other as required.

On the Internet, it can run over different types of networks:

● Local Area Networks (LANs) such as university networks;

● Wide Area Networks (WANs) such as national networks and the wider Internet;

● the MBone (Multicast Backbone), a virtual network layered on top of parts of the Internet, designed for efficient transmission of real-time multimedia using multicast.

In the research and academic world, users will most likely access a videoconference from their networked computer on a LAN connected to the Internet. Many of the tools now appearing are designed for, or adapted to, Internet protocols. ISDN (Integrated Services Digital Network), for which there are many commercial videoconferencing products available, may also be used. There are also products which claim to be usable with a modem connection, 28.8K being the minimum tolerable speed.

ISDN multipoint conferencing using audio, video and/or data is implemented through a Multipoint Control Unit (MCU). The MCU has a focal role in finding a common mode of exchange for the conference participants. It assesses the capabilities of each participant's system and sets a shared technical level at which the videoconference can take place. Such conferences may include features such as voice-activated switching where the focus of the remote window is switched automatically to the person speaking or simultaneous viewing of all conference participants each in their own window. The cornerstone of the negotiation by the MCU is compliance with videoconferencing standards (see further).

Videoconferencing hardware

To use videoconferencing on your networked computer, you will need:

- a video card,
- a camera,
- a full duplex audio card,
- a microphone,
- speakers.

Some systems also require a plug-in (codec) board to handle the compression/decompression. Others use the computer's normal processor plus special purpose software. The hardware solution (the plug-in board) is likely to give better quality, but will also be more expensive.

High-end workstations such as those from Sun, Silicon Graphics, Compaq and HP are well suited to videoconferencing. Many of them have inbuilt facilities for sound, video and multicast access, as well as operating systems and processor power which meet the demanding requirements of quality video. To use a PC for videoconferencing, a 90 MHz Pentium running Windows 95/98 or NT is about the minimum configuration. A good VGA adaptor is necessary for the video display.

Videoconferencing software

There are many videoconferencing applications available both for the high-end workstations and for ordinary desktop computers. A lynchpin of their interoperability is the use of common standards. The main standard for Internet videoconferencing is H.323, and H.324 is the equivalent standard for ISDN. If you are planning to implement videoconferencing software, make sure that the product you choose is compliant to these standards. The use of a common standard is, however, not an absolute guarantee of interoperability. To be quite sure of trouble-free communication, all participants in a conference may need to be using the same tools. More information about standards is available from the International Telecommunication Union Web site at **http://www.itu.int**

See the section below and the 'MBone tools' section for entries on specific tools.

A FAQ about videoconfererencing is available at **http://www.bitscout.com/faqtoc.htm**

CU-SeeMe

CU-SeeMe is one of the most accessible tools providing low-cost desktop videoconferencing. It offers real-time person-to-person or group conferencing on the Internet and intranets. The latest version provides for multiparty conferences of up to 12 people. Multiparty conferences are hosted on a conference server (a reflector) which transmits video and sound to and from all participants. CU-SeeMe can be used with a 28.8K or higher modem connection.

Features:

- color videoconferencing,
- audioconferencing,
- chat,
- caller id,
- whiteboard,
- address book,
- contact list used in conjunction with Microsoft NetMeeting,
- multicast support,
- H.323-compliant.

Access: available from White Pine Software at **http://www.wpine.com**. Versions for Windows 95/98/NT, Macintosh and Power Macintosh.

WebPhone

NetSpeak WebPhone is a modestly priced fully featured phone utility with above average audio quality for this type of tool.

Features:

- full-duplex audioconferencing and videoconferencing,
- firewall proxy support,

- voicemail/answerphone capabilities,

- contacts list,

- conferencing (up to four calls simultaneously),

- caller id information,

- support for personal directory and searching of NetSpeak directory server.

Access: runs on Windows 95/98/NT. Available from **http://www.webphone.com**

Intel ProShare Video System 500

Intel offers this all-in-one system of hardware and software for desktop videoconferencing over ISDN and LAN/WAN. ProShare includes facilities for video, audio, and data collaboration.

Features:

- high quality video up to 30 frames per second,

- full-duplex audio with built-in echo cancellation,

- complies with videoconferencing and data conferencing standards,

- ISDN and Multipoint Control Unit allow linking with associates in other parts of the world,

- LAN bandwidth up to 800 Kbps provides high frame rates,

- integration with Microsoft NetMeeting gives application sharing, whiteboard, file transfer and chat,

- PhotoExchange for capturing and sending images,

- single PCI ISDN/audio/video capture card, headset, microphone, etc.,

- color video camera,

- H323-compliant.

Access: Windows 95/98/NT. Intel Business Video Conferencing page at **http:// support.intel.com/support/proshare/conferencing/**

3.4.4 Audioconferencing/Internet telephony

The future of telecommunications?

The use of the Internet for telephone communications may yet bring a transformation in the telecommunications balance of power, and many telephony services over the Internet offer reduced rate calls which are very competitive. The attraction to the home Internet user is, of course, that while international telephone calls can be very expensive, audioconferencing using the Internet will usually involve a call through the user's modem to their ISP (usually a local call, which may even be free) with the international part being handled by the ISP at no extra charge through to the remote user's computer.

At present though, the available Internet phone tools, though much improved, have not produced a revolution in the way we communicate, one reason being the difficulty of providing the same quality and consistency of the established telephone network across the Internet. Many Internet telephony tools are point-to-point, though at least one allows conferences of multiple calls, and of course if special client software is needed, then each user will need to have the software installed and running. This in itself is a barrier to more widespread use, and it may be that not until Web browsers come complete with reliable audio capability will Internet telephony become commonplace. On the other hand, existing telephone networks and equipment, particularly in the mobile phone market, are increasingly offering Internet services, and the future direction may involve Internet-capable phone devices rather than phone-capable Internet devices! In addition, operators of cable, satellite and other means of delivering interactive TV, radio and telecommunication are all planning the future of integrated media tools which will undoubtedly revolve around the Internet.

Of course, audio is also one aspect of videoconferencing, and many real-time multimedia tools using the Internet offer both audio and video capability. For this reason, this section on audioconferencing is relatively short. A protocol for Internet telephony has been published as RFC 1789 *Using Audioconferencing*. Part of the Internet telephony package is the maintenance of directory lists, both locally and remotely. Many of the vendors of Internet telephony software maintain a server which keeps details such as email address and IP number for users of the service. They also group users according to their stated interests, facilitating contact between users with common interests. Calls are made through the server or direct if the IP address is known. Users need some basic multimedia capability such as a sound card, microphone and speakers/headset.

Audioconferencing tools

Various facilities are available providing audio communication over the Internet. Some are stand-alone packages, others are part of videoconferencing packages (covered in the section above). Some are marketed as a replacement for the telephone system, others are provided as group collaboration services.

Internet Phone

VocalTec's Internet Phone was one of the first on the scene with Internet phone capability and is still a leader in this field.

Features:

- PC-to-PC or PC-to-phone calling,
- audioconferencing support,
- whiteboarding,
- file transfer,
- chat,
- voicemail,
- phone facilities such as caller id, call waiting, etc.,
- personal directory,
- H.323-compliant.

Access: available for Win 95/98/NT, Mac from Vocaltec Communication at **http://www.vocaltec.com/html/telephony/products.html**

Further information

Information about other Internet telephony products is available from: **http://www.iptelephony.org** (select the Clients Phones link).

3.4.5 MBone

The Mbone is a method of delivering real-time multimedia information such as videoconferencing over the Internet. It was a response to the problem of data being chopped up, spliced and left to make its way through variable and narrow routes to its destination, perhaps arriving in time to become one whole again, perhaps not.

The MBone uses a protocol designed to ensure that packets do arrive in time so that the video or audio streams in smoothly. It also addresses the problem of limited bandwidth. The 'M' in MBone stands for Multicast, which is a technique for efficiently 'broadcasting' real-time data over the network without saturating the bandwidth. Only one copy of a multicast message will pass over any link in the network but it will still be available to any (MBone-enabled) local area network which opts to receive it, and from there distributed to users wishing to take part.

Because adding users needn't impose extra load on the network, this technology can support many recipients. Given an adequate supply of bandwidth, it is particularly well suited for real-time multimedia communication. But given that bandwidth on the Internet cannot be guaranteed, quality remains an issue.

The MBone originated in an experiment to multicast audio and video from the Internet Engineering Task Force (IETF) meetings and continued as a medium for research and testing of multicast protocols and services. The potential of multicast technology is beginning to be realized by a wider community and the large and growing body of users now includes commercial sites as well as research and education sites.

Access

In order to use the MBone, you need to be on a network which has multicast routing enabled. The MBone is really a virtual network running over parts of the Internet, connecting up multicast-enabled local networks and workstations, and using its own software, routers and class of IP addresses. MBone sessions may use video, audio, shared whiteboard, text editor, and so on, and IP multicast application software for these will need to be installed. Applications for a number of platforms are available. While Unix workstations have been the norm in the past, most people will begin to use these applications on PCs running Windows. Windows 95 (and later) supports IP multicast; however, the router that connects you to your ISP might not support multicast routing, or the ISP may not be connected to the MBone.

Some of the commonly used applications include:

- **sdr** – session announcements
- **vat** – audioconferencing
- **vic** – videoconferencing
- **wb** – shared whiteboard
- **nt** – text editor.

See the descriptive list of MBone tools below for more information.

Coverage

The MBone can be used for many different types of events and data. Common uses have been to broadcast technical meetings such as those of the IETF. Notable variations from this pattern include the NASA space shuttle launches, a pop concert, courses of lectures, and other live meetings and performances, and developments in streaming media and MP3 over multicast (see below) may also change this technical image.

Multicast technology is well suited to applications in the commercial area too, for example the transmission of stored data streams such as updates of kiosks or video-server-to-video-server updates, as well as transfer of large databases such as stock/commodities quotes and trading information. So called 'push technology' which 'broadcasts' up to the minute information to users such as news or stock prices, is another potential area for multicast development. However, the predominant use of the MBone is currently still with the basic tools developed within the Unix community – sdr, vat etc., and the descriptions in this section reflect that.

Using

Graphical interface

Sdr provides an easy interface for accessing the MBone and all the actions necessary to join a session can be done from here. Its focal point is a menu of sessions currently on offer. A mouse click on one of these enables you to join it and automatically start up the relevant tools for videoconferencing, audio, whiteboard or whatever is being used in the session. When setting up a session yourself, you can check sdr's calendar to see which other sessions are scheduled so as to avoid a clash. You need to provide some basic details on your planned session, decide whether it is to be confined to your site or region or whether it should be worldwide. You can also nominate the format to be used for audio, video, and so on. Once you've made your selections, the planned session will be listed in sdr's menu of sessions and available for others to join.

EXAMPLES

A videoconference of a scientific meeting is announced on the MBone using the tool sdr. MBone users everywhere can use sdr on their MBone-enabled workstation to see the announcement of this videoconference. The announcement will give details of the timing of the conference and the media being used, for example audio, video and shared whiteboard. At the announced time, the broadcast takes place. Interested users will then access sdr again and launch the application software needed for the conference, in this case vat, vic and wb. If they have the appropriate video and audio hardware installed, they will be able to see and hear the speakers in the conference, and see their slides via the shared whiteboard. They will also be able to see a list of other participants in the conference. If the session is opened up for questions, they may be able to ask a question using the audio tool and take part in the subsequent discussion – all in real time.

MBone and streaming multimedia

Streaming media formats such as MP3 are increasingly popular for the delivery of CD quality music and other audio material across the Internet. This is generally not performed using multicast, but the streamed data is sent individually to each user. It is possible, however, to combine the techniques of streaming media and multicast, and tools exist to support this: MP3 players with support for RTP – the Real-time Transport Protocol. Examples are FreeAmp, Audioactive and Winamp, which all have either built-in support or add-ons for RTP. To receive an MP3/RTP stream, you use a 'pseudo-URL' starting with the prefix `rtp://` – i.e. `rtp://<multicast-address>:<port>`

Finding more information

The MBone Information Web at **http://www.live.co/** includes links to information on streaming MP3 via multicast.

MICE National Support Centre User documentation at **http://www-mice.cs.ucl.ac.uk/multimedia/software/** includes links to Installation and User Guides for MBone tools.

Table of multicast-compatible products at **http://www.cs.unc.edu/~wangx/MBONE/mbonetoolarchive.html**

JANET Videoconferencing Advisory Service (VCAS) at **http://www.video.ja.net**

Desktop Videoconferencing – Products and their Interoperability. TERENA Technical report at **http://www.terena.nl/libr/tech/device-fr.html**

Videoconferencing cookbook at **http://www.vide.gatech.edu/cookbook2.0/**

The Virtual Rooms Videoconferencing System at **http://www.vrvs.org**

MBone tools

The following traditional MBone tools require a system which supports IP Multicast connected to an IP Multicast network. Software for these tools can be accessed from the MBone Conferencing Applications page at **http://www-mice.cs.ucl.ac.uk/multimedia/software/**

sdr

Sdr is a tool for announcing and scheduling multimedia conferences on the MBone. Users can use sdr to see what conferences are available and to join them. They can also use it to announce conferences and to specify timing, media and other details. Sessions can be either public or private and may optionally link to further information on the Web.

Features:

- making and receiving session announcements,
- use of encryption for secure session announcements,
- built-in World Wide Web browser.

Access: for information on setting up sdr, see MICE: Installing sdr at **http://www-mice.cs.ucl.ac.uk/multimedia/software/sdr/**

vat

Vat is a real-time, multiparty, multimedia application for audioconferencing over the Internet. While vat is used as an independent audioconferencing tool, it is frequently used as the audio part of a full videoconference.

Features:

- audioconferencing: one-to-one, one-to-many, many-to-many,
- control over local audio,
- details of participants,
- logging.

Access: sound-capable workstation and microphone required. Also the vat software must be installed. See also How to use VAT at **http://www.vrvs.org/Doc/vat-guide.html**; and vat – LBNL Audio Conferencing Tool at **http://www-nrg.ee.lbl.gov/vat/vat.html**

vic

Vic is a videoconferencing tool which provides the video portion of a multimedia conference. Although vic can be run for one-to-one conferences, it is primarily intended as a multiparty conferencing application. It can be used in different computing environments and can accommodate both lower and higher bandwidth conditions.

Features:

- 'Intra-H.261' video encoder,
- voice activated viewing (the viewing window follows the speaker),
- multiple dithering algorithms,
- interactive 'title generation',
- routing of decoded video to external video ports.

Access: VIC User information at **http://www-mice.cs.ucl.ac.uk/multimedia/ software/vic/**. How to use VIC at **http://www.vrvs.org/Doc/vic-guide.html**

rat

Rat (Robust Audio Tool) is an audio tool developed for use in multimedia conferencing. It was designed to be robust to packet loss and adaptive to both host and network conditions.

Features:

- Rat contains features which attempt to compensate for lost and misordered packets.

Access: see the RAT Home Page at **http://www-mice.cs.ucl.ac.uk/multimedia/ software/rat/**. RAT User Guide at **http://www.vrvs.org/Doc/rat-guide.html**

wb

Wb is the shared whiteboard tool. For meetings it provides a normal shared whiteboard on which participants can write, draw and type with all contributions visible to all participants. In a seminar it can be an OHP by using its capacity to import PostScript pages.

Features:

- drawing tools,
- keyboard input of text,
- formatting of text,
- information on other participants,
- import of PostScript pages,
- saving and printing current page,
- multiple pages.

Access: MICE National Support Centre: User Guide to wb at **http://www-mice.cs.ucl.ac.uk/multimedia/software/wb/**. How to use WB at **http://www.vrvs.org/Doc/wb-guide.html**

nte

Nte (NetText editor) is a shared text editor designed to enable a number of people to edit a document simultaneously (though not the same line). It is most appropriate when used as part of a multimedia conference in which it is a support tool.

Features:

● Simultaneous editing of a block of text.

Access: MICE National Support Centre: User Guide to nte at **http://www-mice.cs.ucl.ac.uk/multimedia/software/nte**

Multicast MP3 tools

These tools also require connection to a multicast network, but are primarily Microsoft Windows based, designed for the personal home user, often with digital music as the main motivation. They are essentially MP3 players – tools for playing files in the MP3 digital audio format – but with extended features or add-ons to facilitate more efficient distribution through multicast. Some have versions for other hardware/software platforms.

FreeAmp

MP3 player for Windows or Linux with built-in support for RTP. **http://www.freeamp.org/index.html?mode=features**

WinAmp

AOL/Nullsoft's WinAmp MP3 player (for Windows) can be extended with a free multicast input plug-in which receives MP3/RTP streams and plays them through the WinAmp audio player. **http://www.winamp.com/plugins/**

playRTPMPEG

An MP3 multicast helper tool for Windows and Unix which can enable a non-multicast MP3 player such as Real Networks' Real Player G2 to be used with multicast. The helper tool receives the multicast stream and directs the output to a standard MP3 player. **http://www.live.com/multikit/playRTPMPEG.html**

3.4.6 Streaming

Streaming technology is very popular. It allows high quality multimedia material to be delivered in real time. While much development work is taking place to provide entertainment online, there are also many educational and training applications being developed. A leading company in this field is RealNetworks which provides software to create and play streamed material. Information about RealNetworks is available from **www.real.com**

The technology behind it is that it was not designed to deliver audio and video materials live. When files are sent across the network they are sent in small pieces called packets. These packets can arrive out of sequence and must be reassembled on arrival by the network software. For static files like graphics and text this does not matter and if the user can wait for a whole video or audio file to arrive it can then be assembled and played.

Streaming allows a file to start playing as soon as a small part of it has arrived. This small part of the file, called a buffer, can be a few seconds long. So a user can start to watch a 25 megabyte video file as it is being downloaded or can listen to a radio channel that is playing 24 hours a day (in effect the file doesn't have an end). If you listen to a radio channel on the net and to a traditional radio at the same time you will often notice the delay caused by the buffering.

Streaming can be used to deliver a variety of multimedia formats including audio, video and presentation slides. The RealPlayer plug-in can play all of these simultaneously. The quality of the audio or video being delivered depends on the speed of the network between the user and the server as well as the power of the computer that is being used. A good example of this technology is available from **video.ldc.lu.se/terena.htm**. It provides the presentations and slides from the 1999 TERENA networking conference in Lund, Sweden.

Streaming tools

Real Networks

From their Web site at **www.real.com** you can download their free plug-in to play streaming media. The site also provides software for creating streaming media, RealProducer, and server software for streaming servers.

Apple

The latest version of the popular Apple video format, QuickTime, has built-in support for streaming and does not need to be converted from the .mov format in order to be streamed. Further information is available from **www.apple.com/ quicktime/** including a tutorial on streaming.

Macromedia Shockwave/Flash

A number of Macromedia products are available for use with streaming technology. General information about these products is available from the Web site at **www.macromedia.com**. More detailed information about **'publishing in a streaming format'** is also available.

MicroSoft

The MicroSoft Windows Media Player plays a range of audio and video streaming formats. Further information is available from **www.microsoft.com/windows/ windowsmedia/en/default.asp**

Further information

A good overview of streaming technology is available from **http://www.sec.nl/ persons/ivana/Showcase/intro_streaming.html**

Extended Overview of Video and Streaming technologies and resources: **http:// www.terena.nl/projects/portal/mmis/**

3.5 GROUP COLLABORATION

As the Internet matures, it is increasingly apparent that it is not merely a vehicle for conveying endless amounts of information to the desktop, but that it can also function as an effective platform for working with colleagues, irrespective of their location.

The use of the WWW for collaboration is currently the focus of much interest and development and many interesting new tools are appearing which make online collaborative projects a realistic, if not attractive, option for distributed workgroups. While you can use the Internet for many activities such as holding meetings and ongoing discussions, the definition of group collaboration here is restricted to methods of group working rather than simply communicating, e.g. working together on documents or sharing applications such as a whiteboard.

See also Sections 3.5.1 'Collaborative functions', and 3.5.2 'Software for Collaboration'.

Working on documents

Using collaboration tools, workgroups can jointly edit common documents interactively. For instance, using a whiteboard facility, they might create a project outline for the group, each one contributing points related to their own activities. As it is amended, the display is updated on each participant's computer. When the document is complete, each person can save it for future reference. Alternatively workgroups may need to work on existing documents, for instance spreadsheets or word-processed documents, using application-sharing or document-sharing tools. Another option is to have the document available on the Web and to use an annotation facility to add comments. Collaboration tools provide such possibilities for cooperative work on documents.

Flexible working

The activities discussed earlier, covering both communication and collaboration activities, e.g. holding meetings, discussion forums and working on documents, can be combined with each other, and very often application software will do this for you. Collaboration suites of programs offer various bundled tools accommodating demands for particular combinations. In a videoconference a workgroup might achieve results which would otherwise be out of reach without an outlay of much time and money. As participants confer they can view and work on associated documents and graphics, revising and updating a document in response to comments and suggestions in real time.

In educational situations, a video lecture might be supplemented with complementary graphics or text, for example a manipulable 3-D graphics model, or a slide with expandable bullet points. Students may use audio to ask questions. If video- or audioconferencing are not available or give only poor quality definition, an alternative such as combining chat with document sharing may suffice. Additional functions may be available such as document transfer, annotation of Web documents, group Web browsing, and so on. Most importantly we must analyze our own requirements, then look for tools which might provide what we need. Technology is flexible enough to provide an infinite array for future developments – the only limit is the imagination of Web users/content providers.

3.5.1 Collaborative functions

As we have said above, collaboration via the Internet is currently the focus of much attention and development. New and improved tools demonstrate how workgroups can use the Internet effectively for jointly creating, exchanging or editing documents, sharing a workspace for drawing or brainstorming.

Many of the new collaboration tools are provided on a server and are accessed with a Web browser. Some are also available using browser plug-ins or using special-purpose client software. Collaboration packages provide a whole suite of facilities for collaboration purposes. Combining audio and video communication with facilities such as document and application sharing or whiteboards, provides a powerful mechanism for group collaboration, distance learning and other areas of application.

Some of the new composite tools have been adapted for the Internet from standard groupware applications such as Lotus Notes. Others are new products designed specifically for Internet and intranet use, for example AltaVista Forum. It is notable that the two major browser developers, Netscape and Microsoft, have both been involved with programs for collaboration purposes.

In addition to standard communication facilities such as chat and text/audio/video conferencing which are available as an integral part of many collaborative software packages, the functions found in collaboration tools include:

- document/application sharing,
- whiteboard,
- collaborative browsing of WWW documents,
- annotation of WWW documents,
- voting and rating,
- tracking workflow,
- calendar sharing.

Common collaborative functions

Document sharing

Co-workers can view and edit documents stored in a common area (a shared workspace). Documents are updated as edits occur. Document sharing may simply be a user-friendly interface to uploading and storing of documents on a Web server; however, most document-sharing systems offer a more sophisticated package including management of group members, controls on user access to documents, versioning and annotating. Users may access the system through a Web browser using a password protected area, with some similarities to a Web conferencing area, only here the entries are documents not messages, and have a more complex control system. Examples: BSCW offers shared workspaces for exchanging documents of a range of formats.

Application sharing

In contrast, application sharing involves not the document directly, but the application which is used to create or modify the document. For example, sharing a word processor between two people allows them both to access the menus and functions of the same application to create a single document. This may require each participant to have the application with which the document was produced, such as a word processor or spreadsheet application, or it may be literally sharing one person's application. In this case, only the originator needs to be running the application, and the collaborator merely sees an image of that application sent across the network, but can interact with it as if it were on their desktop. Microsoft's NetMeeting offers application sharing of any applications on the originator's desktop.

Whiteboard

A whiteboard facility allows a group of collaborators to collectively create a document such as a list of priority items, a plan of action or a diagram. The document is edited using mouse or keyboard. Locally the whiteboard program looks like a simple drawing package, but in a live session, changes made to it by any participant appear on every participant's machine. It may be used to support brainstorming, annotation of a diagram, editing and modifying a draft document, etc. Examples: whiteboard facilities are available as part of Microsoft's NetMeeting and the CU-SeeMe videoconferencing tool.

3.5.2 Software for collaboration

SiteScape Forum

SiteScape Forum is an application for group collaboration. It includes a suite of programs for communication and document sharing with flexible provision for controlled access.

Features:

- Web conferencing and chat,
- sharing documents,
- group calendar,
- searching Internet news sources and sharing the results.

Access: Forum runs on a server and is accessed with a Web browser.

Microsoft NetMeeting

NetMeeting consists of a suite of client programs which enable talking (video and audio) and exchanging messages in real time over the net, working on documents and a whiteboard, and exchanging files. Conferences are organized by connecting initially to a directory server.

Features:

- audio- and videoconferencing (two people),
- document/application sharing (three people),
- whiteboard,
- chat,
- file transfer,
- conference switch from one person to another,
- H.323-compliant,
- choice of codec according to line speed.

Access: available free from Microsoft.

Platforms: Windows 95 or NT, and comes as part of the Internet Explorer 5 installation. Video requires a video-capture card and camera. Audio requires a sound card, microphone and speakers. Versions for many languages. See also Microsoft: Complete Communication & Collaboration at **http:// www.microsoft.com/NetMeeting/**

Lotus Domino

Groupware and email server for the Web provide a forum for individuals and groups to collaborate, share information and co-ordinate business activities. Used for building collaborative applications, enterprise-scalable messaging, calendaring and scheduling, and a secure interactive Web site.

Features:

- Web site tools,
- object store,
- search engine,
- dynamic documents,
- managing and securing applications made easy,

- tight security provision,
- replication of information,
- messaging with calendaring and scheduling,
- integration with relational databases through ODBC,
- distribution and tracking of documents,
- agent software.

Access: access to the Domino server is possible with a variety of clients and devices, including Web browsers, Notes clients, and POP3 and other mail clients. Server runs on Windows NT (Intel and Alpha), Sun Solaris SPARC and In tel Edition, AIX, HP-UX, OS/2. For trial purposes, Domino can be downloaded free of charge from the Lotus Notes site at **http://www.notes.net**. Purchase through traditional reseller channels or through Lotus's business partner network.

BSCW

BSCW (Basic Support for Cooperative Work) enables collaboration over the Web. BSCW is a 'shared workspace' system which supports document upload, event notification, group management and much more.

Features:

- shared workspaces for exchanging documents,
- conversion of document formats,
- download and upload via Web browser,
- annotation of documents,
- workspace keeps you aware of changes,
- server available in a number of languages.

Access: to access a workspace you only need a standard Web browser. To create your own workspaces you can use the public server at GMD at **http:// bscw.gmd.de**. Alternatively, you can install your own server at your site. The server software (for Unix or Windows NT) is free and can be downloaded from the BSCW Download page at **http://bscw.gmd.de/ DownloadServer.html**

3.5.3 WebDAV

WebDAV stands for 'Web-based Distributed Authoring and Versioning'. It is a set of extensions to the HTTP protocol which allows users to collaboratively edit and manage files on remote Web servers. WebDAV has been approved by the IETF as a standard. Using WebDAV-enabled tools allows development and maintenance of software within a globally dispersed organization. WebDAV has its own Web site **http://www.webdav.org**

Features:

- locking feature to cope with concurrent writes to the same resource,
- creation, removal and querying of information about Web pages,
- creation, removal and listing of collections of resources,
- version management,
- access control.

Access

Supported in Internet Explorer 5 and other Microsoft products, Apache Web server. See **http://www.webdav.org**. Further information from **http://www.ics.uci.edu/pub/ietf/webdav/intro/webdav_flyer.pdf**

WebDAV software

A wide range of WebDAV products can be found at **www.webdav.org/**

Further information

A good overview of WebDAV, in a presentation format, is available from **http://ceenet.nask.org.pl/workshops99/Miroslav_Milinovits/mmwww399/tsld011.htm**

A wide range of WebDAV resources can be found at **www.webdav.org**

3.6 ftp

ftp (File Transfer Protocol) is a facility for transferring files between host computers on the Internet. ftp really refers to a type of communications protocol, that is, a set of communicating conventions used by the computers involved in a transaction, although people often use the term ftp to mean the ftp software (described below), which uses this protocol.

ftp software

ftp software is freely available from Web, although the ftp protocol is also incorporated into other types of program including Web browsers and Web authoring programs which can also be used to transfer files. A login and password may be required to establish an ftp connection to a 'privately operated' remote computer, although many public archives are available which permit 'anonymous' ftp access by anyone.

Using

Two common uses of ftp are: retrieving software from public archives, and uploading Web documents to a Web server.

Retrieving ('downloading') files

It is possible to put a link in a Web page to a file which can be downloaded by ftp. In this case the user can click on the link, and may be unaware that transfer by ftp is taking place. However, if you see a reference to a file on a public ftp site which takes the form:

```
ftp://domain/path/filename
```

you can type this into the address bar of your Web browser, and this tells it all it needs to know to retrieve the file.

While a Web browser is probably adequate for general day-to-day use, dedicated ftp software such as WS_FTP for Windows, Fetch for Apple Mac, or the Unix ftp program (type ftp <hostname> at the Unix prompt) provides more flexibility and control. For instance, such packages normally allow you to retrieve multiple files in one transaction.

Uploading files to a remote computer

ftp software is often used to transfer files from your local computer to a remote computer. For example, Web pages are often composed on a PC and then transferred using ftp to the Web server, which may be some distance away. Some Web authoring packages include an ftp facility for this purpose. ftp software typically allows you to list, delete or rename files on the remote computer, and to view and alter Unix file permissions.

When logging in to a remote computer to upload files, you may need to specify a logon name and password if you need to access your specific file area rather than the general ftp file area which may be open to all.

Netscape has a basic ftp upload facility built in which is used by typing into the address bar:

```
ftp://username@domain/path
```

General aspects of using ftp

Whichever ftp tool you use, you will need to know the following:

1 The name of the host computer (the domain name or IP address).
2 The location of the file (the path).
3 The filename.

When an ftp connection is established using a client program, a username and password will be asked for. If it is a computer on which you have an account, you will need to supply your usual username and password. For public ftp sites the following convention is used: log on with the user id 'anonymous' and enter your email address as the password. Once successfully logged on, you may then need to specify one of two modes of transfer:

● ASCII (plain text),
● binary.

You may not need to alter this setting unless you discover that files are not transferring successfully. Use the ASCII transfer option for plain-text files such as HTML files, PostScript and anything produced with a plain-text editor. Use binary for other file types such as word-processed, database, spreadsheets, graphics, compressed files or executables. If binary files are transferred in ASCII mode, the transfer may not be successful and the file may be corrupted. Some ftp software can automatically detect the correct setting.

EXAMPLES

Downloading a file from a public ftp archive with a Web browser

The file wsftp32.zip is located in the public directory /pub/mirror/win95/winsock-l/FTP/ on the ftp server ftp.uni-magdeburg.de. To ftp it using a Web browser, type the following into the address bar:

```
ftp://ftp.uni-magdeburg.de/pub/mirror/win95/winsock-l/FTP/
ws_ftp32.zip
```

Depending on how its preferences have been set, the browser will save the file to your disk, unzip it for you, or ask you what you would like done with it.

Using Netscape to upload files

You can use a Web browser to upload files to your own filespace on a server. Suppose you have a username xenon on the ftp server sun1.ucs.tam.org and your directory is /user/xenon. In the address bar of your browser, type:

```
ftp://xenon@sun1.ucs.tam.org/user/xenon
```

You would then be prompted for your password, and when that has been accepted, be presented with a Web page listing the items in that directory. You could then transfer files into the directory by dragging and dropping their icons into the page. If you don't mind sending your password in the URL, alternatively you could do this in one step by using:

```
ftp://xenon:password@sun1.ucs.tam.org/user/xenon
```

4

WEB PUBLISHING

This chapter explains how to author Web pages and publish them on the Web. All Web pages are written in a special language called HTML, but there are different ways of producing HTML: by writing it directly, using an authoring tool, or converting from another format (e.g. Word documents). Whatever method is used it is helpful to understand something of the basics of the HTML language.

When you have written Web pages, how do you 'publish' them on the Web? To do this, the finished HTML file(s) need to be transferred to a computer which is connected to the Internet and which operates as a Web server.

Topics covered include:

- Web authority
- Publishing Web pages
- Graphics in Web pages
- Multimedia
- Interactive Web pages
- Web databases
- XML

4.1 WEB AUTHORING

All Web authoring tools produce HTML, but the tools differ in the range of features and facilities they offer. In addition to HTML generation, Web authoring software commonly includes facilities for managing whole sets of Web documents. Also common are ready-made templates and graphics to enable rapid development, wizards to help get novices going quickly, help with generating scripts, styles, graphics, animation, etc. Beginners should probably start with one of the simpler authoring tools and then move on to more advanced software.

4.1.1 Web authoring tools

There are dozens if not hundreds of authoring tools available; many are free but the most expensive can cost several hundred dollars. Beginners are often put off by the bewildering choice. However, the difference between authoring tools at beginner level is relatively unimportant – it is much better to pick one and learn it than waste time and money seeking the 'best' tool. Among professional Web authors there is no widespread agreement on the 'best' tool and like any type of software individual preference has a lot to do with it. Practically all the commercial products offer free trial versions – so you should try out software before buying it.

Many Web authors continue to write HTML by hand using a text editor, partly because this offers maximum control, and partly because they are reluctant to spend time learning an unfamiliar tool which may prove unsatisfactory. Whatever tool is chosen, it is helpful if not essential to understand a little about the HTML language. Most authoring tools have minor quirks which may require manual viewing or editing of the HTML in order to correct it.

Authoring tools fall into two main types: basic HTML tools which require the user to understand HTML, and WYSIWYG (what you see is what you get) tools which hide the details of the HTML.

WYSIWYG authoring tools

Using WYSIWYG tools is similar to using a word processor, and they hide the details of the HTML from the user. Many authors use both the WYSIWYG interface and some 'raw' HTML authoring. However, the HTML code produced by some of these tools may not conform to the correct standards. This could mean that your page is not displayed properly. WYSIWYG editors also allow you to insert and position images into a page. You can certainly produce a page much quicker using a WYSIWYG tool than by writing HTML, but you should check that the HTML code produced by the tool is of an acceptable standard.

More advanced tools may offer features in addition to simple Web page authority. Some of these are discussed below.

A good review site about Web authoring tools is **webreview. com**

Automatic navigation

Good authoring tools can automatically create links between the pages in your site, and keep them up to date as you add or remove pages. This is much quicker than manually editing links.

Site mapping

Authoring tools with site mapping features display a graphical representation showing how all your pages are linked and how these links connect to external sites.

Site management features

Facilities to manage your site: link checking, HTML validation, global find and replace, global 'themes' or House Style, simple upload to the server.

Inclusion of other technologies

Authoring assistance/templates for JavaScript, Cascading Style Sheets, ASPs (Active Server Pages), inclusion of Java applets.

Finally, some tools also allow you to produce dynamic pages which normally require other programming technologies. For example: database connectivity, password authentication and processing of forms data. However, the important thing to note here is that for the dynamic pages to work, these tools require special software installed on your Web server. Beginners using this type of authoring tool may create dynamic pages only to find that their service provider or institution does not provide the necessary software on the Web server. Examples are: ColdFusion, FrontPage ('FrontPage Extensions' need to be installed on Web server) and Drumbeat.

Basic authoring tools

Netscape Composer is built into later versions of Netscape (**www.netscape.com**) and is a basic WYSIWYG editor suitable for beginners. Many other basic tools are available from freeware/shareware sites such as **www.tucows.com** and **www.winsite.com**. Microsoft Frontpage Express is a basic Web authoring tool which is included with later versions of Internet Explorer.

Popular authoring tools

Name	Available from	Comment
HotDog Professional	http://www.sausage.com	
Adobe Pagemill	http://www.adobe.com/products/ pagemill/main.html	Originally Mac software
Allaire Homesite	http://www.allaire.com/Products/ HomeSite	Integrates with other Allaire products
BBEdit	http://www.barebones.com/ products/products.html	Mac only
HoTMetaL Pro	http://www.hotmetalpro.com	
Dreamweaver	http://www.macromedia.com/ software/dreamweaver	Integrates with other Macromedia products
FrontPage 2000	http://www.microsoft.com	Some features depend on special Web server configuration

Complex authoring/site development tools

Name	Available from	Comment
Visual InterDev	http://www.microsoft.com	
Drumbeat	http://www.macromedia.com/ software/drumbeat	
ColdFusion	http://www.allaire.com/Products/ coldfusion	NT and Unix versions

Validating HTML

If Web authors wish to provide pages that are accessible to the widest possible audience, they should check that their HTML conforms with current standards. This process is known as **HTML validation**. Information on the current standard is available on the Web site of the **World Wide Web Consortium http:// www.w3c.org/**

HTML editing programs commonly provide an HTML validation function, and may even enforce conformance to standards as the HTML is generated, e.g. **HoTMetaL Pro**. Alternatively documents can be run through an HTML checking program, either locally, or by using an online service such as:

- Online testing of HTML
  HTML Validation Service http://validator.w3.org/

- Online testing for broken links, invalid HTML, and server response time
  NetMechanic: Online Link Testing, HTML Validation
  http://www.netmechanic.com/

- Online testing for CSS
  CSS Validation Service **http://jigsaw.w3.org/css-validator/**

For entries on specific tools, see above.

4.1.2 HTML: HyperText Markup Language

HTML is like a hidden layer behind the document that you see in a Web browser. It is, as its name implies, a **markup language**. Marking up text is like issuing instructions on how the text should be interpreted and displayed. In the case of HTML, the instructions come in the form of HTML **elements**, or **tags**. The Web browser displays a document as instructed by the HTML. HTML tags do a number of things, such as the following:

- **define the structure of a document**, for example the HEAD (information about the document) and BODY (the main part of the document which is displayed by the browser)

  ```
  <HEAD>
  <TITLE>Title of the document</TITLE>
  </HEAD>
  <BODY>
  This is the main body of the document.
  </BODY>
  ```

- **indicate features of the appearance**, for example white background and blue text

  ```
  <BODY BGCOLOR="WHITE" TEXT="BLUE">
  ```

- **indicate formatting of text**, for example text in italics

  ```
  <I>HTML elements</I>
  ```

- **indicate the presence and position of graphics**, for example show the image file box.gif here and place it on the left of the page

  ```
  <IMG SRC="box.gif" ALIGN="LEFT">
  ```

HTML files are plain-text (ASCII) files. The filename will have the extension `.html` or `.htm`. To see the HTML source of a Web document, select the browser's View/Source menu option. There are many programs which can help in generating HTML, and also a number of the programs we are accustomed to using (such as word processors) now include a function for automatically generating HTML.

Creating Web pages is not merely a technical exercise. Good style and good practice have an impact on the quality and usability of pages. Check out the Bibliography for useful guides for Web authors which cover issues of style, as well as HTML.

For a summary of HTML elements, see:

- *Barebones Guide to HTML* **http://werbach.com/barebones/** by Kevin Werbach. Brief reference listing of the most common HTML tags. Available in a number of languages.
- *Sizzling Jalfrezi HTML* **http://vzone.virgin.net/sizzling.jalfrezi/iniframe.htm** HTML tags defined, discussion of techniques, abundant examples and references.

The full HTML standard is available from the WWW Consortium site at **http://www.w3c.org/**

Other types of file

Although HTML is the normal format for Web pages, files in any format can be made available on the Web, leaving the user to handle the details of viewing or processing files. Web browsers now contain plug-ins which can automatically display common file formats such as PDF (Portable Document Format). You can also configure your browser to handle other common file formats such as Microsoft Word. For other file formats the user can download the file and then run whatever software is necessary outside of the Web browser.

4.2 PUBLISHING WEB PAGES

As a minimum, a Web page consists of a single HTML file. In practice, most Web pages also include some associated image files (.gif, .jpg, etc.). To publish a Web page the finished file(s) need to be transferred to a Web server. A Web server is a computer which is connected to the Internet, and which has special Web server software installed. How you transfer your files to the Web server depends on local circumstances, but typically this is done in one of the four ways described below.

Directly to a mapped drive

You may be able to connect your computer to the Web server if it is on your local network. For example, on a PC you may be able to set up drive w: as a direct connection to the server. Ask your network administrator.

ftp

ftp (File Transfer Protocol) software is used to transfer files between two computers. ftp software is freely available and may be provided by your Internet Service Provider or network administrator. You log on to the remote computer by entering your user name and password, and then you can transfer files.

Via a Web page

If you have Web space with a commercial Internet Service Provider, some companies allow you to upload your files using your Web browser. Their Web site will have an 'upload page', where you enter your logon name and password details, and then you are presented with a dialogue box asking for the name(s) of the files to upload.

Web authoring tool

Web authoring tools often have a built-in facility to transfer files, which connects directly with the Web server.

Announcing your site

There is little point in having a site which no one visits, so potential visitors need to be given a way of discovering the existence of your site. The first step is to optimize the site's findability with the popular Internet search services. You do this by registering it with major search engines such as AltaVista, Excite, Infoseek, Lycos, Hotbot, etc. and with directories such as Yahoo!. Also, if there are relevant specialist directories, let them know too. Most search engines and directories will provide an obvious and inviting link to their site registration page. Alternatively you can pay a service to do it for you such as Submit It! (**http:// submitit.linkexchange.com/**). In either case, search engines will put your URL into a lengthy queue which their spider will eventually visit for the purpose of collecting data for the search engine's index. Once your site is in the index, in theory it can be found by keyword searching. With directories such as Yahoo!, the important item in your submission is the description of your site which will be processed, not by a program, but by a person, who makes the decision on whether or not to include it in the directory.

Guidelines for optimizing findability with search engines:

- With each Web page, come straight to the point with concise, descriptive text for the title and headings and also the first paragraph. Use words which are directly relevant to the subject of the document. With some search engines, the words used early in the document are more significant for findability than those used later, but repeated occurrences of words and phrases also influence findability (beware of index spamming!).
- Insert meta-tags for keywords and description into the head of your documents, particularly pages which are framesets and pages which start with JavaScript.

Maintaining your site

Publishing information on a Web site should not be regarded as a one-off process – if you want people to return you need to put in a lot of time and effort to keep your site up to date. Check hypertext links regularly to make sure that they still work. There are many free tools available for doing such housekeeping tasks automatically. Also read and revise the text if necessary. From time to time, you may wish to review the style too (how impressed are you today by a page of plain black text on a grey background!).

Usage statistics are an important aspect of maintenance. They will tell you, for instance, if anyone is accessing the information you are providing or if they encountered errors in finding any of the files you linked to. Some statistics packages also track the route that users follow through the site.

4.3 GRAPHICS IN WEB PAGES

Graphics play an important role in Web pages, in enhancing their appearance, aiding navigation through a site, helping to create a style or corporate image and providing illustration. Some of the issues which Web authors need to understand are: which image formats to use, how to optimize images for the quickest possible download, 'Web-safe' colors and how to create animated gifs.

4.3.1 Image formats

There are two main formats which are supported by popular browsers. These are:

- GIF
- JPEG.

An emerging format is:

- PNG (Portable Network Graphics).

GIF and JPEG formats are supported by all graphical Web browsers. The GIF format is most suitable for line-art images such as icons, graphs and line-art logos. JPEG is better for photographic images. One major difference is in the number of colors supported. GIF supports up to 256 colors, while JPEG can use 16.7 million colors. GIF is actually a proprietary format owned by CompuServe. The PNG format was created as a non-proprietary alternative to GIF, and contains some improvements, e.g. better compression and more control over transparency. PNG is supported in later versions of Netscape and Internet Explorer.

GIF

The *Graphics Interchange Format* or GIF is a common image format used in Web pages. It was originally developed by CompuServe. There are two versions of the GIF format: versions 87a and 89a. Features:

- **File compression** The GIF image format uses a built-in LZW compression algorithm, for which Unisys Corporation holds the patent. Commercial vendors, whose products use the GIF LZW compression, must license its use from Unisys, but end-users do not need to pay to use GIFs.

- **Transparency** While both GIF formats support transparency, Version 89a also supports background transparency. This means that the background of an image can be made to appear the same color as the background of the Web page, a standard technique on Web pages.

- **Interlacing** Interlacing allows for progressive enhancement of the image as it loads, rather like the way in which a view through a window is revealed by a gradually opening Venetian blind.

- **Animated GIFs** *Animated GIFs* are actually a compound image consisting of a set of separate images displayed at timed intervals, thus providing the effect of animation. The GIF89a format includes enhancements which make this possible.

JPEG

JPEG stands for Joint Photographic Experts Group. It is commonly used for graphics in Web pages and is a particularly effective glossy compression method for natural, photographic-like true-color images.

- **Progressive JPEG** A progressive JPEG is transmitted and displayed in a sequence of overlays, with each overlay becoming progressively higher in quality.

4.3.2 Efficient and effective images

One of the most important aspects of the usability of Web graphics is the efficiency with which they can be displayed. Download time is dependent on the size of the image file. Many Web authoring programs provide a facility which estimates the graphics' download time. A rough estimate can be made on the basis of 1 Kb per second over a telephone line. Some Web developers striving for maximum impact aim to keep total page size below 50 Kb or less.

Three factors govern the size of an image file: using the appropriate format for the type of image, reducing the physical size of the image, and reducing the number of colors used. Photos should be saved as jpegs. Images should be cropped to remove any unnecessary detail, and the size of the image should be reduced to as small as possible. If a full sized illustration is required, create 'thumbnail' images which show the user what the image looks like before they download the full size one. Finally, reduce the number of colors used in the image to a minimum. Practice with an image editor will show how many colors are needed for different types of image before quality is affected.

Note that the height and width attributes of the HTML IMAGE tag only affect how the image is displayed – the download time is the same irrespective of how big it is displayed.

The use of color palettes helps to strike the right balance between efficiency and image quality. Palettes may be based on the colors which occur most frequently in the image, on the colors to which the human eye is most sensitive, and in the context of the Web, the Web-safe palette.

Web-safe palette

Different browsers and different computers process colors differently, so that it is impossible to be sure that the colors you see on your screen appear the same for all users. Browsers which cannot reproduce a color exactly attempt to match that color with an approximation which may make your site look unpleasing. This mechanism is called 'dithering'.

The 'Web-safe' palette consists of 216 colors which will appear consistently on both the Apple Mac and Windows platforms, so many authors use this palette as a starting point when creating images for the Web. Web graphics packages usually allow you to specify using a browser-safe palette.

4.3.3 Imagemaps/clickable images

Imagemaps or 'clickable images' are images on a Web page which are used as navigation aids; specific areas of an image are linked to related Web pages which the user accesses by clicking on them. Imagemaps are usually written in HTML, by coding the co-ordinates of the different areas and their related Web pages into the HTML page on which the image is displayed.

Many authoring tools (including freeware/shareware tools such as MapEdit) provide a facility for creating the necessary HTML code and image co-ordinates, because to work out the co-ordinates is tedious and impractical. When the user clicks on a spot in an image, the Web browser 'knows' where the user has clicked, and displays the related page. This is known as 'client-side' imagemapping.

Early versions of Web browsers did not support this method of implementing imagemaps, but there is an alternative method which involves a CGI program running on the Web server. When the user clicks on an image, the co-ordinates are sent to the CGI program which delivers the related page. This method is known as 'server-side' imagemapping. Normally there is no longer any reason to use this method, because client-side imagemapping is easier and requires no programming.

See Section 4.3.4 below for entries on a selection of graphics packages.

4.3.4 Graphics software

DeBabelizer Pro

This tool specializes in automating repetitive tasks in high-volume graphics production for Web, print, and multimedia delivery.

Features:

- automated file conversion,
- easy creation of scripts for batch processing,
- ready-made scripts for common tasks,
- easy creation of palette for a group of images,
- compilation of GIF animations.

Platforms: Apple Mac, Windows 9X/NT.
http://www.equilibrium.com/

Fireworks

This high-end suite of tools from Macromedia aims to provide a unified environment for creating, optimizing and producing high-quality graphics for the Web. It includes tools for text, design, illustration, image editing, URL, JavaScript, and animation and is closely integrated with Macromedia's Dreamweaver.

Features:

- import, optimize and preview with a range of formats,
- works with both vector and bitmap images,
- multiple layer support,
- image slicing,
- Web-specific color features,
- GIF animation tool,
- visual export preview,
- control over compression and color palettes,
- automatic generation of button states and JavaScript rollovers.

Platforms: Windows 9X/NT, Apple Mac.
http://www.macromedia.com/software/fireworks/

GIF Construction Set for Windows

This is special-purpose software (shareware) for creating transparent, interlaced and animated GIF files for Web pages.

Features:

- easy interface to creating transparent GIF files,
- builds GIF files through drag and drop,
- animation wizard tool,
- banner, transition and LED signs options,
- supercompresses GIF files,
- flips, rotates, scales and crops all or part of an animated GIF file.

Platforms: Windows 3.x/9X/NT.
http://www.mindworkshop.com/alchemy/gifcon.html

GifBuilder

This is a utility to create animated GIF files on the Macintosh.

Features:

- can collect PICT, GIF, TIFF or Photoshop images,
- can convert QuickTime movies, FilmStrip or PICS files,
- outputs GIF89a file with multiple images,
- Version 0.5 features frame icons in the Frames window,
- filters,
- transitions,
- animation cropping.

Platforms: For Apple Mac.
Available from **http://mac.simplenet.com/graphics/gifbuilder/**

Graphic Workshop Classic

This shareware general multifunctional graphics package comes from Alchemy Mindworks, Inc.

Features:

- batch convert between most popular image formats,
- view, crop, resize, rotate, print and process graphics,
- create thumbnails,
- PNG, GIF89a, JPEG, and MPEG and QuickTime viewing supported,
- displays a slide show of images,
- image filters,
- image database with keyword searching.

Platforms: Windows 3.x/95/NT.
http://www.mindworkshop.com/alchemy/gww.html

ImageReady

ImageReady from Adobe is especially designed for Web graphics production. It contains a subset of Photoshop features, but includes some extras particularly suitable for the Web.

Features:

- optimized colors palette,
- simultaneous views of image (optimized, compressed and dithered vs. uncompressed),
- neat handling of transparency,
- GIF animation palette,
- image slicing,
- imagemaps,
- JavaScript actions,
- batch handling,
- easy interface.

Platforms: Windows 9X/NT, Mac.
http://www.adobe.com/prodindex/imageready/main.html

MapEdit

MapEdit is a graphical editor for World Wide Web imagemaps (clickable imagemaps).

Features:

- easy creation of client-side imagemaps,
- supports GIF, JPEG and PNG formats,
- will also create server-side maps for backwards compatibility with old browsers.

Platforms: Windows 3.x/95/NT, Unix, Apple Mac.
http://www.boutell.com/mapedit/

Paint Shop Pro for Windows

This is a shareware graphics editing, viewing and conversion package.

Features:

- supports over 30 image formats,
- numerous drawing and painting tools,
- dockable tool bars,
- enhanced selection options,
- built-in special effects filters,
- RGB color separation,
- animated GIF.

Platforms: Windows 9X/NT.
http://www.jasc.com/pspdl.html

Painter Classic

Painter is a digital painting tool which can be used to add effects to existing images or create images from scratch.

Features:

- simulates traditional artists' tools such as paint, chalk, etc.,
- extensive brush library,
- tools to increase efficiency,
- flexible intelligent brushes,

- apply filters to existing images.

Platforms: Windows 9X/NT, Power Mac.
http://www.metacreations.com/products/

Photoshop

Adobe Photoshop is a professional package for photo design and production with a rich array of functionality and a well-established reputation for creation of high quality graphics.

Features of the latest version:

- support for multiple layers in images,
- enhanced color control,
- flexible tool for adding type to images,
- history palette,
- task automation and batch processing,
- professional photography tools,
- assortment of painting and drawing tools,
- sophisticated selection capability,
- multiple options in user interface,
- filters,
- transformations,
- multilanguage support.

Platforms: Mac, Windows, Unix.
http://www.adobe.com/prodindex/photoshop/

4.4 MULTIMEDIA

The term 'multimedia' is used in different ways. In one sense ordinary Web pages are a multimedia environment, because they can contain a mixture of text, still and video images, sounds, and animations and they are interactive. However, in this context most people use multimedia to mean additional software/technologies which generally require proprietary authoring software to create, and appropriate plug-in/helper software to view/hear. There are many competing products to author multimedia applications (both for the Web and outside of it), as well as others which are used to deliver video and/or audio. This section introduces common terms/tools.

A related topic is SMIL (Synchronized Multimedia Integration Language) which is a language specification produced by the W3C. SMIL allows the co-ordination and combination of different multimedia elements, e.g. sound, video, Web pages etc. Experimental SMIL browsers have been developed, and parts of SMIL have been implemented in Internet Explorer 5.0 and above.

In the continuing quest for maximum impact with minimum wait, formats and techniques which advance the goal of efficiency attract continuing interest from developers. For instance in the area of animation, there is increasing recognition of the benefits of standards and tools (e.g. Flash) based on vector graphics rather than bitmap formats. Also, as compression techniques improve, traditional tools formerly associated with large files (e.g. QuickTime) now boast more speedy downloads of super-compressed files. One of the great current success stories on the Internet is MP3 (MPEG Audio Layer 3), an efficient compression standard for audio files giving near perfect sound quality with economical file size.

There is also added flexibility in the ways in which multimedia is handled. Tools such as RealPlayer which process streaming audio and video (played as it downloads) have made the playing of live audio and video broadcasts an everyday reality on the Internet. This streaming facility complements the traditional mode of *local* playback where files need to be completely downloaded before playback can begin. Animation, and in particular, user-activated animation, is fast becoming a standard feature in Web pages and many new tools have emerged in this area. Meanwhile the tried and tested animated GIF continues to flourish.

Dynamic HTML, though still not implemented evenly across browsers and platforms, is a major factor in shaping the appearance and interactive functionality of the Web, employing JavaScript and style sheets for user-activated animated effects.

With advances in compression techniques and tools, the use of the Internet as a distribution medium for recorded music has burgeoned, vastly increasing the scope for piracy. Tools such as Liquid Audio seriously address both technical and intellectual property issues related to CD-quality music distribution.

Providing multimedia

Multimedia content can be incorporated into Web pages with HTML using the following tags:

- `APPLET` Used to embed Java applets.
- `EMBED` tag Used for any file type using Netscape plug-ins (Navigator 2+, Internet Explorer 3+).
- `OBJECT` tag General solution for dealing with new media. Recommended by the W3C and incorporated into the HTML 4.0 specification (also backward compatible).
- `BGSOUND` Used to embed background sound files (Internet Explorer).
- `ANCHOR` tag Used to link to multimedia files outside the current document.
- `IMG` Used for animated GIFs.

Also using Microsoft proprietary attributes (Internet Explorer only):

- VRML virtual worlds with the VRML attribute;
- AVI (Audio Video Interleave) video clips with the DYNSRC (Dynamic Source) attribute.

The `APPLET`, `EMBED`, `OBJECT`, `IMG`, and `BGSOUND` tags automatically initiate the display or playing of file or object when a page containing them is loaded. If the object is a streaming-media type, playing will begin as soon as a certain number of bytes have been received and will continue as the file is downloading. If it is not streaming, playing cannot begin until it is fully downloaded, which in the case of large files, runs the risk of having it aborted by an impatient user. To make sure the page is viewed with or without the multimedia object, a low-risk alternative is to offer the option of playing the file by providing a link to it with an `ANCHOR` tag, preferably with descriptive text.

Usability

Web developers using multimedia need to look carefully at usability issues. Users will not be impressed by multimedia if it requires them to spend time installing software or if it takes a long time to download. Do not use multimedia as a substitute for content. Consider what percentage of users already have the required software, either because it is widely distributed or is a standard browser plug-in. Ensure you provide a link to the source of the software. Using a plug-in to play the file may mean that the user cannot save your content for later.

Playing multimedia

Multimedia content is played via plug-ins or helper applications. See Section 4.4.1 below for entries on a selection of popular tools. Recent browsers now have plug-ins/helpers pre-installed for many common multimedia formats, for example LiveAudio comes as part of Netscape and requires no additional downloading or configuration.

When a plug-in application is required, normally it can be downloaded for free, and in many cases requires little intervention on the part of the user, although manual configuration is sometimes necessary.

4.4.1 Multimedia software

Cosmo Player

Cosmo Player, which comes as a Netscape plug-in or ActiveX control, is a universal player for VRML 2.0 content. Cosmo Player 2.1.1 requires ActiveMovie 1.0 or later in order to support video and compressed audio within VRML worlds. It uses Direct-Sound3D, available in DirectX 3.0 or later, to provide realistic, spatialized audio.

Platforms: Windows 9x/NT/2000: **http://www.platinum.com/cosmo/win95nt.htm**
Mac OS 7+: **http://www.platinum.com/cosmo/mac.htm**

Flash

Flash is a tool for creating browser-independent multimedia content for the Web including text, animation and sound. It uses vector graphics rather than pixel-based graphics, so files are modest in size, but still capable of high impact. Flash is widely distributed, being currently included with Internet Explorer and Netscape Navigator.

Platforms: Windows 3.x/9X/NT/2000, Mac OS 8.5, 8.6, 9.X.
http://www.macromedia.com/software/flash/ (look for authoring program)

Liquid Audio

A particular feature of the technology of Liquid Audio is the facility for publishing CD-quality music via the Internet with built-in security features for protection of the intellectual property rights of artists and labels. Liquifier Pro, the software for preparing the content, provides professional tools for digital sound processing plus the capability to include lyrics, credits and artwork. Watermarking, which identifies authentic copies of the music, inaudibly embeds digital data into the audio file.

Platforms: Mac, Windows 9X/NT/ME/2000.
http://www.liquidaudio.com/

LiveAudio

Player for sound files in a range of formats including .aiff, .wav, .au and MIDI. Included with Netscape Navigator 3.0 and higher. Includes a player console to stop, start, pause and adjust volume.

Platforms: Windows, Mac.
http://www.netscape.com/navigator/v3.0/audio.html

MGI Viewer

MGI Viewer is a mixed media viewer for high-resolution Flashpix images. Features include zoom, viewing of 360-degree panoramic images, viewing 3-D image objects from all angles, audio, video and URL links. Content is created with tools such as PhotoVista, PhotoSuite, Reality Studio and Live Picture Image Servers.

Platforms: Windows 9X/NT/2000, Mac OS.
http://www.mgisoft.com/support/downloads/plugin.html

QuickTime

QuickTime supports digital video formats like QuickTime VR, AVI, AVR, DV and OpenDML, and uses video compressors and decompressors to optimize the quality of streaming video, making this technology accessible even at modem speeds. It includes state-of-the-art technologies to maximize video quality while maintaining the smallest possible file size. QuickTime player is included with Netscape Navigator 4.0 and higher.

Platforms: Apple Mac, Windows.
http://www.apple.com/quicktime/

RealPlayer Plus G2

RealPlayer Plus G2 delivers live and on-demand real-time RealAudio and RealVideo streaming content on the Web, promising broadcast quality at even modest modem speeds. It provides controls for tuning audio and video quality. G2 technology reduces rebuffering, which means less break-up in RealAudio and RealVideo streams. For information providers, RealVideo is a scalable cost-effective media server solution making possible the broadcast of multiple simultaneous video streams.

Platforms: Macintosh 68K, Macintosh Power Mac, Windows 3.x/9X/NT/2000, OS/2, IRIX, Sun Solaris, and Linux.
http://www.real.com/

Shockwave

The interactive multimedia Shockwave player is freely available as a Netscape plug-in or ActiveX control. Shockwave supports combinations of audio, animation, video, real-time interactivity and 'live' objects. The files are created with Macromedia Director, a high-end complex multimedia authoring program with its own scripting language. Shockwave uses highly-developed MPEG compression to optimize the quality/file size ratio.

Platforms: Shockwave ships with Windows 95, 98, 2000, MacOS, Internet Explorer CD, America Online, and Netscape Navigator.
http://www.macromedia.com/shockwave/

Windows Media Player

This player delivers most of the main audio and video formats including ASF (Advanced Streaming Format – its native format), WAV, AVI, MPEG, QuickTime, and others. It can be used for playing anything from low bandwidth audio to full-screen video, including streaming video. At the server end, the Windows NT Server NetShow Services provides for creation, storage and streaming of live and on-demand content.

Platforms: Macintosh, Windows.
http://windowsmedia.com/download/download.asp

Further sources of multimedia plug-ins and helper applications

Plug-In Plaza (all media) **http://www.browserwatch.com/plug-in.html**
3-D Graphics Software **http://www.webreference.com/authoring/graphics/software/3d.html**

The VRML and Java3D Repositories at Web3D Consortium **http://www.web3d.org/vrml/vrml.htm**

4.5 INTERACTIVE WEB PAGES

This section presents a selection of the many ways of producing interactivity in Web pages.

The default process by which documents are delivered on the Web is an inherently static one:

1 A client requests a document at a particular Web address (URL).

2 The server at that location fetches the requested document (e.g. an HTML page, an image, etc.) and transmits it back to the client.

3 The document is displayed by the browser on the client machine.

There are a variety of methods available for making the Web more interactive and in order to introduce dynamic behavior each of these stages can be enhanced or altered.

In the browser, Dynamic HTML, JavaScript, Java and ActiveX controls can affect the display of the document. All the processing that provides the interactive behavior is actually performed by the browser. This is often referred to as client-side processing.

In contrast, technologies such as ASP (Active Server Pages), CGI (Common Gateway Interface) and SSI (Server Side Includes) dynamically influence the page each time it is requested from the server, i.e. server-side processing. This is a tremendously powerful means of generating pages which are always up to date and adapt themselves to the user's requirements. Because the processing is taking place on the server before the page is delivered to the browser, the results will appear the same, regardless of the client browser type or computing platform. Such techniques are employed with great effect in the development of database-driven Web sites.

One complication of these server-side technologies is the implication for caching and indexing of documents.

Cookies assist with session and user tracking and involve both client and server in a limited way.

The topics covered in this section are:

● **Dynamic content and caching**

- **Dynamic HTML** The combination of HTML, style sheets and scripts that allows documents to be animated.

- **Java applets** Java byte-code pulled across the network and executed by the browser when the appropriate tag is encountered in an HTML page.

- **JavaScript** Programs embedded inside an HTML page are executed on-the-fly by the browser.

- **Common Gateway Interface** A standard for fetching Web documents generated dynamically by the Web server.

- **Active Server Pages** A server-side technology from Microsoft used for creating dynamic Web pages.

- **Server Side Includes** A means of dynamically including content in a Web page. The included content may be files (e.g. header and footer files), server-generated information (e.g. current date, date of last modification, date of the document), or the output of a CGI script (e.g. hit counter).

- **Cookies** Small pieces of data created by servers and stored at the browser for later use.

Distributed object technology

Software component models, such as CORBA (**http://www.omg.org/ gettingstarted/**) and DCOM (**http://msdn.microsoft.com/library/backgrnd/html/ msdn_dcomarch.htm**) provide a framework within which distributed software objects can communicate with each other, regardless of location or platform. The consequence of these component models for the Web is that they offer a means to easily integrate software components in order to generate new applications or to extend old ones. For example, browsers, protocols or commercial applications, with the added benefits of all the sophisticated distributed systems services and techniques that are available within the model can be used collectively.

Existing products that use these technologies are **Javabeans** and **ActiveX**.

4.5.1 Dynamic content and caching

Caching of Web pages considerably speeds up retrievals, whether it is handled by the user's browser, a local proxy server, or a regional or national caching service. However, with dynamically generated pages the benefits are not as clear-cut as with static pages. If a dynamic page is retrieved from the originating server and stored in a cache, when the user retrieves it from the cache some time later, they may not see the page as it is meant to be seen. This may be because the information is no longer current, or it is not the version of the page for the browser they are using, or another variation is determined by server-side processing. On the other hand, if pages always need to be retrieved from the originating server, the user does not benefit from the speed and access improvements offered by caches, particularly where connectivity is poor.

When these issues have been weighed up, the Web protocol (HTTP) offers the content provider a means of exercising control over how long their pages are cached. If freshness of content of dynamically generated documents is the main priority and the document should not be cached at all, this can be specified in the header by setting the 'Expires' value to zero. Alternatively, the value could be set to one day, one week, or whatever is appropriate. Conversely, where the provider (using an Apache Web server) wants to make sure that documents containing SSIs are cachable, a tool called xbithack can be used.

Dynamically generated pages also have implications for search engines. Here it is not a question of freshness of content, rather of stale indexing. Index terms collected by the search engine may no longer apply when the document is accessed some time later. One ameliorating factor is that frequently updated pages tend to attract frequent visits by search engines, and consequently, frequent updates of their index.

Further information

Information Resource Caching FAQ: **http://www.ircache.net/Cache/FAQ/**

4.5.2 Dynamic HTML

'Dynamic HTML' is a collective term for a set of technologies which produce Web pages which are responsive to user actions. The appearance or content of the page can change in response to actions such as mouse clicks or movements, keying in text, or other keyboard actions. Although not yet fully implemented in all browsers, Dynamic HTML represents a leap forward in the potential for client-side interaction.

Dynamic HTML is made up of three key elements:

- **Cascading Style Sheets (CSS)** CSS gives authors greatly enhanced control over the presentation of the Web page by separating document display information from the actual content. With CSS it is possible to specify attributes such as text color, margins, alignment, font size, etc.

- **Scripting languages** Scripts in languages such as JavaScript are embedded in the HTML page and interpreted by the browser as it loads the page. They are typically used to generate responses to user events such as mouse clicks, form input, and page navigation.

- **HTML tags** The HTML 4.0 specification provides tags to embed objects and scripts, and to support style sheets.

Other associated features of Dynamic HTML are:

- **Content positioning** Content positioning allows for precise alignment and layering of blocks of HTML content such that they can be exposed, hidden, moved, expanded or contracted in response to user actions.

- **Downloadable fonts** Any font required to enhance a Web page can be incorporated into the page and is downloaded on demand if required by the client browser.

DOM

The foundation for Dynamic HTML is the Document Object Model (DOM). The DOM defines the anatomy of the page. Within a hierarchical framework, each element within a document can be specified. There is for example the document itself, the head, the body, links, images, text styles, etc. Elements and styles also have their own properties. For instance a table has height and width, a heading has a font style and font size. The DOM provides the framework by which these elements and their style properties can be accessed and manipulated by client-side scripts.

The World Wide Web Consortium has issued the DOM Level 1 Specification as a W3C Recommendation, thus defining a standard API (Application Programming Interface) that allows authors to write programs that work without changes across tools and browsers from different vendors.

Using Dynamic HTML

Because the DOM allows client-side scripts to access style elements and their associated properties it is possible to alter the appearance of objects in a Web page in response to user actions (events). For example, the style of a link could change when the mouse is moved over it.

CSS enables absolute positioning of HTML elements, using exact x, y, and z co-ordinates. It is therefore possible to animate precisely positioned content, for instance to move an object to a different position on the page when it is clicked.

Unfortunately Dynamic HTML is inconsistently rendered by the fourth generation Netscape and Microsoft browsers. This is mainly because they currently implement the DOM in a slightly different way. Netscape Navigator 4.0 gives scripting languages less access to page elements than Internet Explorer. For example Netscape Navigator 4.0 cannot change style properties after the page has loaded.

Another difference between Netscape and Internet Explorer is in the implementation of content positioning. Netscape uses the LAYER tag while Microsoft bases its approach on a combination of Cascading Style Sheets (DIV and SPAN tags), Active X, and its own Document Object Model.

EXAMPLE   *Rollover*

In this example, two style classes are defined using CSS. This STYLE declaration is placed in the HEAD of the document:

```
<STYLE>

.on        {
           font-size: 16;
           font-style: italic;
           font-family: san-serif;
           text-decoration: none;
           color: red;
           }

.off       {
           font-size: 16;
           font-style: normal;
           font-family: serif;
           text-decoration: none;
           color: blue;
           }

</STYLE>
```

In the document, scripts are used to apply these class styles to objects in a dynamic way, that is, in response to user actions. Employing the JavaScript functions *onMouseOver* and *onMouseOut* the object changes style when the mouse is moved over it (in this case, the object is an empty link):

```
<A HREF = "#"
CLASS = "off"
onMouseOver = "this.className ='on';"
onMouseOut = "this.className = 'off';">
Example of a rollover
</A>
```

The result

Due to the different implementation of the DOM between browser types (see above) this example will only work correctly using Microsoft Internet Explorer. Move your mouse (without clicking) over the text below; it should change as you do so.

Example of a rollover

Finding more information

Dynamic HTML Lab: **http://www.webreference.com/dhtml/**

Web Review – What is so Dynamic About Dynamic HTML? **http://www.webreview.com/1998/07_24/webauthors/07_24_98_1.shtml**

Inside Dynamic HTML: **http://www.insidedhtml.com/**

Netscape DevEdge Online: **http://developer.netscape.com/tech/dynhtml/index.html**

Project Cool Dynamic HTML Developer Zone: **http://www.projectcool.com/developer/dynamic/**

4.5.3 Java

Java is a programming language from Sun Microsystems designed to run in a secure manner on any platform without modification of the source code. These characteristics make it ideal for developing network applications – programs that you can download from a remote machine and execute on your own computer. The most common use of Java on the Internet is in the form of applets which can be executed by Java-enabled Web browsers. Java's built-in security mechanisms aim to prevent inadvertent or malicious interference by the applet with any other part of the user's system.

Using

Java applets can be run by any Java-enabled browser, such as HotJava from Sun Microsystems, Netscape Navigator and Internet Explorer. The applet program is dynamically loaded across the Internet and executed inside the Web browser when the browser encounters an <APPLET> tag in an HTML document.

The basic components needed to write applets or stand-alone applications in Java can be downloaded for free in the form of Sun's Java Development Kit (JDK) from JavaSoft (**http://www.javasoft.com**). This includes the core class files, a compiler and an interpreter. There is a useful tutorial at **http://www.javasoft.com/docs/books/tutorial/index.html** at JavaSoft which covers both basic and specialized aspects of using the language.

It is also possible to download and use ready-made applets from one of the many public archives available on the Web.

EXAMPLE   Sun Microsystems gives examples of Java technology in action at **http://www.javasoft.com/nav/used/index.html**

Developers may find the Java resources in the Java Repository at **http://java.wiwi.uni-frankfurt.de** useful.

Finding more information

The *JavaWorld magazine* is an online magazine aimed mostly at programmers which contains lots of technical information and discussion about Java.

4.5.4 JavaScript

JavaScript is a client-side scripting language used for writing small programs that are embedded inside a page of HTML. As the page loads the JavaScript code is interpreted by the browser. JavaScript was developed at Netscape, and is recognized as standard by Microsoft's Internet Explorer as well (although Microsoft originally developed its own version of JavaScript called JScript).

By operating on the client side, JavaScript speeds up simple interactive behavior without needing to use the network. For example, simple verification of the data entered into a form (e.g. numbers only in telephone field) could be carried out in the browser via JavaScript inside the HTML of the form page. This reduces server load and speeds up performance at the client side. In general, the use of an embedded client-side scripting language can create a more event-driven page, reacting instantly to user input such as mouse clicks or text entry at the browser.

Using

Scripting languages such as JavaScript commonly function as a key component in the technology of Dynamic HTML. Using Dynamic HTML, properties of objects in the Web document can be accessed and manipulated, generating interactive and animated pages at the client end without recourse to interactions with the Web server.

To run a program written in any scripting language, your browser must be able to interpret the particular language that is being used. Both Netscape and Internet Explorer browsers can execute JavaScript programs.

Examples of JavaScript abound on the Web. Many can be found at **http:// www.developer.com/directories/pages/dir.javascript.html**

EXAMPLES

The tutorial at **http://rummelplatz.uni-mannheim.de/~skoch/js/tutorial.htm** is a useful introduction to JavaScript.

Finding more information

See the Netscape documentation on JavaScript at **http://developer. netscape.com/ docs/manuals/index.html** and the Microsoft Scripting Technologies page at http://msdn.microsoft.com/scripting/default.htm

4.5.5 Common Gateway Interface

The Common Gateway Interface (CGI) provides a standard interface between Web servers and other, external programs and applications. For example, using CGI to access a database means that non-WWW information can be made available via the WWW. It is a server-side technology in which the processing of information takes place at the server end and the results are sent back to the Web browser in a dynamically generated HTML page generated on-the-fly.

Using

The typical CGI scenario is:

1 The user clicks on a link in a Web page which represents the URL of a CGI script, e.g. submitting a database search request.
2 The request is sent by the browser to the Web server.
3 The Web server executes the CGI script, e.g. a database search for the keyword.
4 The script sends HTML output back to the server and terminates.
5 The dynamically generated HTML page containing the output is displayed by the browser.

A document generated using CGI will be indistinguishable to the requesting browser from a normal static Web document (although the content of the page and its URL may make its origins evident). Because CGI documents are created on demand they cannot be cached locally. In order to reload the same page the CGI script will need to run again on the server and regenerate the document.

The use of CGI on a Web server is usually strictly controlled by the server manager, because of the security risks inherent in effectively allowing anonymous users to execute programs on the system. To create the actual scripts or programs that do the work, any programming language can be used. Popular choices are interpreted languages such as Perl, PHP or Python, although compiled languages such as C and Visual Basic can also be used.

For collections of sample programs see:

● CGI Resource Index **http://www.cgi-resources.com**
● Matt's Script Archive **http://www.worldwidemart.com/scripts**

EXAMPLES   Examples of CGI programs are widespread on the Web: counters, forms, guest books, imagemaps and interfaces to database collections. See a collection of examples at **http://www.developer.com/directories/pages/dir.cgi.html**

Finding more information

The W3 CGI page at **http://www.w3.org/pub/WWW/CGI/Overview.html** contains links to more documentation and discussion about CGI.

4.5.6 Active Server Pages

Active Server Pages or ASP is a server-side technology from Microsoft for building dynamic and interactive Web pages. ASP code is embedded in the HTML page. When such a page is requested from the Web server, the server first executes the ASP instructions, then constructs the page including any ASP-generated information, and returns it to the client. ASP is similar in concept to CGI.

Using

By default Microsoft Web servers (Internet Information Server 3 and above) can run ASPs (may need to install/configure the server software to do this). Other server types (e.g. Apache) can be ASP-enabled using third-party tools such as chilisoft! from **www.chilisoft.net**. ASP pages are browser independent.

ASP code is usually written in a language called VBScript which is embedded inside the HTML on a page within <% and %> tags. ASP pages (with extension .asp) can contain any combination of HTML and script commands.

ASP uses an inbuilt set of objects and components to manage specific aspects of interactivity between the Web server and browser. Objects include the Request (made to the server), the Response (returned by the server) and the Session (allows the user's visit with the Web site to be treated as a continuous action, rather than a series of disconnected page requests).

Active Server Components provide ready-made functionality. Examples include database access, determining browser capabilities, linking to and writing into text files.

ASP scripts are text files and can be written by hand in any simple text editor. Tools are also available. Visual InterDev provides a fast way of building ASP scripts. Also some general Web authoring programs such as Microsoft FrontPage and Allaire HomeSite enable you to create and edit ASP scripts. Drumbeat provides a drag and drop interface to the code creation.

EXAMPLES Here is a simple example of the use of a conditional statement in responding to an order confirmation from the user:

```
<%
If varOrderConfirm = "Yes" then
    Response.Write "Your goods will be despatched within two
weeks."
Else
    Response.Write "Your order was not confirmed."
End If
%>
```

But the potential for interactivity goes a great deal further than this. For instance, ASP can be used to customize the Web page for the individual user providing a selection of topics which interest the user, and indicating what is new since their last visit. It could also be used to link an online store to an existing inventory database and order-processing system.

Examples of large sites using ASPs:

- Microsoft **http://www.microsoft.com/**
- Dell **http://www.dell.com/**
- Gateway **http://www.gateway.com/**

Finding more information

Microsoft: Active Server Pages at **http://msdn.microsoft.com/library/tools/aspdoc/iiwawelc.htm** and **http://www.microsoft.com/OfficeDev/Index/ASP.htm**

Microsoft: Active Server Pages Tips and Tricks at **http://www.microsoft.com/AccessDev/articles/ASPT&T.HTM**

Also see useful resources at **http://www.learnasp.com/**

4.5.7 Server Side Includes

Server Side Includes (SSI) is a means of creating a 'template' Web page, which places some standard text in a set of Web pages or applies a consistent appearance across a set of Web pages.

Using

The HTML/text which is to be used as a template is saved in one file, and then each individual page contains a special instruction to include this file.

If the Web author wants to change the appearance of an entire site, then only the template file need be changed.

When the user types a URL for a Web page, the Web server software dynamically creates a 'final' page which includes whatever is in the template (hence 'server side'). Because this mechanism happens at the Web server end, and is invisible to the user, any Web browser may be used. Server Side Includes is a feature of the Web server software; Apache and Microsoft IIS both support it. Syntax differs slightly depending on the Web server used.

EXAMPLES

Suppose you wished to include the following HTML in all the Web pages on your site:

```
<H2>
<IMG SRC="logo.gif">
University of London</H2>
<I>email: webmaster@lon.ac.uk<I>
```

You would save this in an ordinary text file called e.g header.inc. By convention SSI template files are often saved with the .inc file extension.

In order to include the above HTML in a Web page, the following syntax would be used:

```
<!-#include file="header.inc"->
```

Server Side Includes can also be used to dynamically insert other information such as local time, date or file information (filesize, filename, creation date, etc.)

Finding more information

Introduction to SSIs: **http://www.carleton.ca/~dmcfet/html/ssi3.html**

A book by Ben Laurie and Peter Laurie: **http://www.webreview.com/1997/10_10/developers/10_10_97_7.shtml**

About Apache Server Side Includes: **http://www.apacheweek.com/features/ssi**

4.5.8 Cookies

Cookies are a way of saving information from the Web server on the browser. A cookie is a small amount of data that is sent by the server the first time a user accesses the site and it is stored, by the browser, on the user's computer. When making requests the browser checks whether a cookie has previously been saved for that site and if so, sends the cookie back to the server along with the request for the page.

The contents of a cookie can be anything the server wishes to 'remember'. It must have an expiration date and is limited in size. Cookies have often been perceived as a security risk and possibly an invasion of privacy.

Access

Cookies are not something to which you would normally require access. They are used by browser and server to help personalize your Web usage; for Web site managers, cookies are a useful way of monitoring individual usage and preferences.

However, if you should want to see what information is being collected on your behalf, the file or files are located on the same computer as the browser you use, and possibly in the same directory, though their location can vary with different browsers.

Microsoft Internet Explorer stores cookies in a directory inside the user's local profile directory. Netscape appends new cookies to a single file called cookies.txt. It is possible to transfer cookies from one browser to another.

Using

A WWW user may not be aware that cookies are being set by the sites he or she is visiting, although some browsers may be configured to warn the user before accepting a cookie, or even not allow the cookie to be set. For example Netscape 4 provides options of accepting all cookies, accepting none, or accepting only cookies which are sent back to the originating server. Similar options are available in other browsers.

The option Accept only cookies that get sent back to the originating server effectively excludes cookies to be sent to third-party servers – such as those which provide banner advertising on popular sites, e.g. Doubleclick.

Since the data is stored on the client computer, a user can always delete or corrupt the relevant files if they do not wish to keep the cookies.

Scripts are written using CGI or JavaScript.

Common uses of cookies include tracking which pages are visited by a user at a particular site over multiple visits, storing information such as name and password, or, at a site consisting of a sequence of ordered pages such as a training course, remembering where the user reached on his/her last access. In the commercial context, cookies may be used to store information on items ordered, the usual analogy being the shopping trolley to which items are added at intervals, with a final tally being made by reference to cookies.

EXAMPLES

Finding more information

An excellent overview of cookies is at Cookie Central **http://www.cookiecentral.com/index.html**, and there is another at Andy's Netscape HTTP Cookie Information **http://cgi-resources.com/detail/00277.html**

The Cookie specification (draft RFC) can be found at **http://portal.research.bell-labs.com/~dmk/cookie.html**

4.6 WEB DATABASES

As the Web becomes a mainstream technology for all sectors and particularly commercial enterprises, there is a growing interest in Web/database integration driven from two main sources:

- the desire for a cross-platform, easily accessed interface to legacy databases;
- the requirement for up-to-date information on large, complex and constantly changing Web sites.

Interface to legacy databases

When a database and Web site are integrated, database users do not need to have access to the database application, nor are they limited by computing platform or location. With a system of password entry, they can securely carry out traditional tasks such as data entry and retrieval using just their Web browser.

Dynamic Web sites

For a Web site containing rapidly changing information it is not practical to continually rewrite HTML pages to cope with the demand for up-to-date content. By using a database to store and generate Web site content, the Web server uses SQL (Structured Query Language) queries to get content automatically from the (constantly maintained) database and dynamically creates the Web pages. Dynamic generation can be carried out as the page is requested. Where heavy traffic would make the load of the database too great or for pages that update less frequently, the HTML pages can be generated en masse at regular intervals and posted on the site as regular pages.

The drawbacks of dynamically generated Web sites are the implications they have for indexes (such as search engines) and caches. See Section 4.5.1 'Dynamic content and caching' for a discussion of the issues.

Web database application server

There are a variety of tools to choose from when setting up a Web/database system. It is only necessary to find an affordable combination of operating system, Web server, database management system, and the tool which acts as the interface between the Web server and database.

The interface technology could be:

- a custom application written in Perl, Java, etc., accessed through CGI;
- Active Server Pages (ASP) running on the Web server;
- a specialized third-party Web database application server such as ColdFusion;
- part of an all-in-one package such as Oracle.

A Web database application server interfaces with the Web server through its Application Programming Interface (API). API extensions installed on the server extend the server's capabilities to use other technologies.

Database management system

Most of the database systems likely to be used in Web services will be ODBC (Open DataBase Connectivity), which is a compliant relational database queried with SQL. ODBC handles the connection between the Web server and the database as well as the translation of requests. ODBC drivers are available for many database systems. (JDBC is the equivalent standard for use with Java-based applications.) Popular desktop database systems are Microsoft Access, FoxPro,

FileMaker Pro. Examples of enterprise level systems are Oracle, Ingres, Sybase, Informix, DB2, Microsoft SQL Server, MySQL.

Enterprise level systems have the requisite power, speed, and security protection to cope with multiple, concurrent users and transactions. Desktop database systems are less complex but may be adequate for most uses, particularly for an intranet or a low-traffic Internet site.

See also Section 4.6.1 below.

4.6.1 Web/database tools

Active Server Pages

http://www.microsoft.com/OfficeDev/Index/ASP.htm

See also Section 4.5.6. ASP is a server-side programming technology from Microsoft which can be used for developing a Web interface to an ODBC (Open Database Connectivity) database. Built-in ActiveX data objects link the database to the Web server and ASP Web pages access and manipulate data from a Web browser.

ASPs may be authored using an authoring tool such as Drumbeat or Microsoft Visual InterDev.

ColdFusion

http://www.allaire.com/products/coldfusion/index.cfm

A popular cross-platform Web application tool, ColdFusion provides a fast way of building and deploying applications integrating browser, server and database technologies. It uses a tag-based scripting language (CFML) that integrates with HTML and XML which is processed by the ColdFusion Application Server. It boasts scalable deployment and high performance even on demanding sites, security features, and extensibility with a wide range of technologies. It includes built-in support for Oracle and Sybase, as well as general ODBC support.

Filemaker Pro

http://www.filemaker.com/

FileMaker Pro is known as an easy-to-use data-sharing database for the end-user. Its new ODBC import function allows querying of ODBC data sources and import of the results. Originally Mac software, there is now also a PC version.

MySQL

http://www.mysql.com/

MySQL is a very fast, multi-threaded, multi-user and robust SQL database server. For Unix and OS/2 platforms, MySQL is basically free; for Microsoft platforms you must get a MySQL license after a trial time of 30 days.

MySQL is often used as a database backend integrated with the Web using PHP3 or CGI scripts.

Oracle

http://www.oracle.com/ip/deploy/database/8i/

Oracle8i is specifically designed as an Internet development and deployment platform. It combines the functions of database server, Web server, file server and application server. It includes a Java Virtual Machine and has implemented support for SQLJ, an embedded SQL language for Java.

PHP

http://www.php.net

PHP is a scripting technology/language with syntax similar to C, Java and Perl. Originally developed for the Unix platform, there are now versions for Windows, Unix and Linux. PHP is an **opensource** project which means by definition that it costs nothing to use.

SQL Server

http://www.microsoft.com/sql/

SQL server is an enterprise level database product which is designed for large-scale use, and as a Microsoft product can be easily integrated with a Web site using ASPs.

Tango

http://www.pervasive.com/products/tango/

An industrial strength tool for creating Web applications using backend databases, Tango includes Development Studio and Application Server. Tango will support any ODBC-compliant database as well as direct connections to Oracle, Butler SQL and FileMaker Pro, and is available for many platforms.

4.7 XML

What is XML?

XML (eXtensible Markup Language) is a new development in the evolution of (markup) languages for creating Web/Internet content. It uses tags in a similar style to HTML but allows users to create their own tags.

However, there are important differences between XML and HTML. Whereas HTML is used to control the format or appearance of a page of text, XML is used to define the structure and processing of data. This can provide important advantages in the management and retrieval of information, and separates stylistic issues from the content. HTML contains a strictly defined number of tags which cannot be changed or extended; XML allows Web authors/information providers to create their own set of tags for individual purposes. Strictly speaking XML is a 'meta-language'; that is, a language which is used to define new languages with strict rules about the structure and formatting of information written when using them.

Advantages of XML:

- additional flexibility – to create new tags;
- separation of presentation and content – better information management;
- built-in error checking and validation;
- built-in processing features, e.g. to sort or search data;
- can be used to exchange data between applications;
- complex hierarchical data structures possible;
- more precise search and retrieval of data possible.

Example of XML document

EXAMPLE

Suppose you wish to structure the play *Macbeth* as XML. It might look something like this:

```
<?xml version="1.0"?>
<play>
<playtitle>Macbeth</playtitle>
<act number="1">
<scene number="1" location="a desert heath">
```

```
<directions>Thunder and lightning. Enter three
witches.</directions>
<line person="first witch">When shall we three meet again? In
thunder, lightning, or in rain?</line>
</scene>
</act>
</play>
```

Note that the rules of XML are stricter than HTML. For example, HTML allows single tags without a closing tag e.g. `<HR>`, but XML insists on every element being properly closed. Also, XML is case sensitive. Notice an important difference between HTML and XML: there are no formatting instructions here as there would be in HTML.

eXtensible Style Language (XSL)

The details of how the individual elements are to be formatted in an XML document are stored elsewhere – either using cascading style sheets, or another type of language called XSL – eXtensible Style Language. XSL is similar in concept to CSS, but is more complex (XSL contains programming constructs which can be used for processing/sorting data). Without the style sheet instructions, browsers would not know how to display the content.

Keeping the formatting instructions separate from the structure and content of the XML document gives two main benefits:

- content and style can be altered without affecting each other or the structure of the document;
- alternative styles can be presented for different environments. For example, a style for printing rather than screen display, or a style for display on a mobile phone rather than a Web browser.

Document Type Definitions (DTDs)

It is possible to define the exact rules for an XML structure in what is called a Document Type Definition (DTD). A DTD specifies which tags are nested within other tags, in what order they can be used, and which parts are optional or compulsory etc.

A DTD can then be used to validate XML documents.

XML Schema

XML Schemas express shared vocabularies and allow machines to carry out rules made by people. They provide a means for defining the structure, content and semantics of XML documents.

XML Schema has recently (2 May 2001) been approved as a W3C Recommendation (**http://www.w3.org/XML/Schema**). XML Schema Specification consists of three parts:

- **XML Schema Part 0: Primer** is a non-normative document intended to provide an easily readable description of the XML Schema facilities, and is oriented towards quickly understanding how to create schemas using the XML Schema language. XML Schema Part 1: Structures and XML Schema Part 2: Datatypes provide the complete normative description of the XML Schema language. This primer describes the language features through numerous examples which are complemented by extensive references to the normative texts.

- **XML Schema: Part 1: Structures** specifies the XML Schema definition language, which offers facilities for describing the structure and constraining the contents of XML 1.0 documents, including those which exploit the XML Namespace facility. The schema language, which is itself represented in XML 1.0 and uses namespaces, substantially reconstructs and considerably extends the capabilities found in XML 1.0 DTDs. This specification depends on XML Schema Part 2: Datatypes.

- **XML Schema: Part 2: Datatypes** defines facilities for defining datatypes to be used in XML Schemas as well as other XML specifications. The datatype language, which is itself represented in XML 1.0, provides a superset of the capabilities found in XML 1.0 DTDs for specifying datatypes on elements and attributes.

Implications of XML

If one considers ordinary pages of textual information, XML can be used as a more efficient way of managing and structuring information. This can lead to important advantages in terms of information management (less duplication/redundancy, greater accuracy, more control over revisions, error checking, providing different formats/versions of information for different circumstances).

However, XML has the advantage that it can be used to create and structure other forms of information – e.g. abstract languages such as music, mathematics or chemistry. Such information can then be displayed, processed in other ways (e.g. playing music, displaying 3-D molecules), or used as a format to exchange data with other applications. None of this is possible using an HTML-type approach.

On the other hand, in the early stages it is much harder to define and construct an XML page or DTD and specialist/abstract applications as described above since they require substantial technical/programming skills.

Examples of XML applications

- MathML (Mathematics Markup Language) **http://www.w3.org/TR/REC-MathML**
- CML (Chemical Markup Language) **http://www.xml-cml.org**
- SMIL 2.0 (Synchronized Multimedia Integration Language) **http:// www.w3.org/ TR/smil20/**
- Blocks Extensible Exchange Protocol (beep) **http://www.ietf.org/ html.charters/beep-charter.html**

XML browser compatibility

- IE4: partial support for XML, reasonable CSS
- IE5: good support for XML and CSS
- Netscape 4: no XML, moderate CSS support
- Netscape 5: good support for both XML and CSS.

XML developer tools

- Creating DTDs at DevGuy XML **http://www.devguy.com/fp/XML/dtd.htm**
- Apache XML Project **http://xml.apache.org/**
- XML Spy – Integrated Development Environment including XML editing and validation, Schema/DTD editing and validation, XSL editing and transformation **http://www.xmlspy.com/**
- A Conversion Tool from DTD to XML Schema **http://www.w3.org/2000/04/ schema_hack/**
- The Microsoft XML Parser (MSXML) 3.0. Features: server-safe HTTP access, complete implementation of XSL Transformations (XSLT) and XML Path Language (XPath), changes to the Simple API for XML (SAX2) implementation, including new SAX2 helper classes, even higher conformance with W3C

standards and the OASIS Test Suite, a number of bug fixes. **http://
msdn.microsoft.com/xml/general/xmlparser.asp**

References

- W3C's XML HomePage: **http://www.w3.org/XML/**
- XML Schema: **http://www.w3.org/XML/Schema**
- XML Protocol Working Group: **http://www.w3.org/2000/09/XML-Protocol-
Charter**
- XML Homepage: **http://www.xml.com/**
- XML.ORG – independent resource for news, education, and information about
the application of XML in industrial and commercial settings at
http://www.xml.org/

5

SECURITY AND ENCRYPTION

The use of the Internet for electronic commerce, electronic publishing, distributed private databases, teleworking, collaborative working, online education, virtual meetings, and so on holds exciting promise. But some of these uses rely on the security of electronic transactions for their widespread viability.

Security, or the fear of security problems, is one of the main obstacles to the adoption of Internet technologies to some commercial applications, and it lies behind the reluctance of many consumers/customers/users to make widespread use of the Internet for shopping, online banking and other commercial activities. In fact, security is not an important issue for many of the general-purpose uses of the Internet – for gathering and supplying information which is intended for public consumption. Reliable security is, however, essential for the transmission of sensitive and commercial data on the Internet, whether it is between individuals or companies, employers and employees, vendors or purchasers. Security on the Internet is now a big issue and much effort is being invested in developing a security mechanism which addresses current needs and concerns.

There is much misunderstanding of what the security issues are, and where they are relevant. The current Internet infrastructure, for example, has no security mechanisms built into it, primarily because the Internet was not designed for these commercially sensitive applications, but merely for general or academic information interchange. Reliable security methods do, however, exist in many of the tools and technologies which we use on the Internet, for example in email applications or Web browsers. In general, Internet users do not make use of these security mechanisms (and don't know how to), and should not assume that they are in place unless it is explicitly stated. This chapter outlines some of the security issues and available solutions. At the heart of most of the solutions is encryption – the method of transforming text into a coded message so that it is not readable by unauthorized users. Encryption and its uses, therefore, feature heavily in this chapter.

Topics covered include:

- Security issues
- Encryption
- Security on the Web
- Secure email
- PGP
- SSH

5.1 SECURITY ISSUES

Security risks

Many security risks associated with the Internet are, in fact, general security issues relating to general working practices or the use of computers, such as passwords detailed below. The Internet does, however, alter some of the means and methods of unauthorized access. In particular, the computer users are often no longer operating in isolation, but have potentially opened up access to their computer systems to a much wider user base. The most common areas in which the Internet can be seen to have increased or added security risks are:

- 'hackers' – people attacking the computer systems remotely;
- speed and ease of access is increased;
- transmission (and detection) of viruses is more rapid and widespread;
- easy transmission of data worldwide (accidental/deliberate);
- easy technical solutions for 'e-stealing';
- poorly configured Internet systems leave loopholes.

In terms of hackers, there are a variety of sources of attack to networked computer systems, categorized by the motives of the attacker:

- joyriders – who do it for fun;
- vandals – acting maliciously to cause damage;

- score keepers – who compete with peers on the challenge of hacking;
- spies (industrial and otherwise) – who set out to steal valuable information.

Finally, there is stupidity and accidents: '55% of all security incidents actually result from naive or untrained users doing things they shouldn't' (Richard Power, *Current and Future Danger: A CSI primer on computer crime and information warfare*, San Francisco, CA: Computer Security Institute).

Maintaining a secure environment

First, some general guidelines relating to maintaining the security of your account (that is, your login and password on an Internet host, and associated access to filespace, electronic mailbox and Web space). To a large extent users rely on system managers to take care of the overall security and integrity of the system. However, if hackers are intent on breaking in, any weakness in the system can provide an initial entry point. This can be provided by a single user who is slack about the security of his or her id and password.

- Keep your password secret. Don't give it to anyone else, and especially, don't include login and password details in an email message.
- Use a password which can't be guessed or found in a dictionary.
  Recommended practice is to make it a mixture of letters and numbers, upper case and lower case.
- Change your password frequently. Normal computer security is important for network security. Network login details may be obtained from your computer if it falls into the wrong hands.
- Keep your computer secure. Don't leave a machine on which you are logged in unattended.

Security requirements

In exchanges of data, there are a number of basic security requirements. Special measures designed to meet these requirements need to ensure the following:

- Confidentiality – the data cannot be read by any unauthorized person.
- Integrity – the data has not been tampered with in transmission.
- Authenticity – we can be certain of where the data originates.

Remember: CIA!

Encryption is integral to meeting these needs and forms the basis of many of the tools for security and privacy, such as PGP and SSH. This chapter looks at some of these tools, in particular ones that relate to user requirements, rather than those specific to the security concerns of Web site administrators or system managers. Two obvious areas of interest are ensuring the privacy of email, and maintaining the security of transactions via the Web. In fact there are a number of types of security, depending on the situation, the type of information, and the information/ service provider and the users. These include:

- confidentiality – keeping information 'secret';
- data integrity – stopping the information being altered;
- availability – ensuring a service is provided continuously;
- consistency – maintaining the same service without alteration;
- control – restricting access to information;
- audit – being able to track back to a previous known stable state of the data.

Organizations naturally attach importance to different types of security, for example in the banking environment integrity and auditability might be more important than confidentiality and availability. However, in areas of national defense, classified information will frequently be involved, leading to confidentiality being the first concern and possibly availability the last.

Finding more information

Computer security and computer security incident response

Rainbow Series Library: **http://www.radium.ncsc.mil/tpep/library/rainbow/**

The Common Criteria VERSION 2.1/ISO IS 15408: International Common Criteria Project Home page: **http://www.commoncriteria.org/**

CERT/CC: **http://www.cert.org/**

Information page on Computer Security Incident Response at TF-CSIRT at TERENA: **http://www.terena.nl/task-forces/tf-csirt/sec-idinfo.html**

Security software

For extensive lists of security software, see:

- TERENA TF-CSIRT page on Tools and Software for Intrusion Detection and System Security: **http://www.terena.nl/task-forces/tf-csirt/sec-idtools.html**

Federal Computer Incident Response Capability: **http://www.fedcirc.gov/ tools.html**

CERT List of Security Tools: **http://www.cert.org/tech_tips/security_tools.html**

DOE Information Security Custom Tools: **http://doe-is.llnl.gov/SecRes/ DOECustomTools.html**

SANS Institute's 'The Network Security Roadmap': **http://www.sans.org/ newlook/publications/roadmap.htm**

5.2 ENCRYPTION

Encryption is one half of cryptography, and together with the other half – decryption – allows the coding and decoding of text into and out of a form which is undecipherable. Encryption, then, is the process of using a key (cipher) to scramble readable text into unreadable ciphertext, that is, text that can only be read by someone with the cipher for decrypting it. Encryption on the Internet has many uses, from the secure transmission of credit card numbers via the Web to protecting the privacy of personal email messages. Authentication also uses encryption, by using a key or key pair to verify the integrity of a document and its origin.

Methods of encryption

Single key encryption (conventional cryptography) uses a single word or phrase as the key. The same key is used by the sender to encrypt and the receiver to decrypt. Sender and receiver initially need to have a secure way of passing the key from one to the other, and as such the use of this method is limited.

Examples include IDEA (International Data Encryption Algorithm), DES (Data Encryption Standard), RC2 and RC4 (used in international versions of software such as Netscape Navigator).

Public key encryption uses two types of key for secure encrypted communication: a public key, which may be freely given out to others, and a secret key, which is known only by you. Thus, for secure communication, a total of four keys is required:

- the sender has a public key and a secret key,
- the receiver also has his or her own public key and secret key.

Using public key encryption to send a message is a three-step process:

1 Sender and receiver exchange their public keys (their secret keys are never given out).
2 The sender uses the recipient's public key in encrypting a message for sending.
3 The recipient's complementary secret key is used to decrypt the received message.

Note that once the message has been encrypted using the recipient's public key, even the sender will no longer be able to decrypt the resultant encrypted message. An example of public key encryption is RSA, the original public key encryption system invented by Rivest, Shamir and Adelman.

Keys

Cipher keys come in various sizes (measured in bits), generally the bigger the better, though public cipher keys usually need to be longer than single cipher keys to achieve the same level of security. While 128-bit single key encryption provides an acceptable level of security, encryption with a 40-bit key may not necessarily withstand a concerted effort to break the code. Single key encryption systems provide an efficient method of encryption but they present no foolproof way of securely exchanging keys. Public key encryption gets around this particular problem. Public keys are intended to be distributed openly, and collections of public keys are available on public key servers. Note that public key servers do not undertake to check the authenticity of keys stored in their databases.

Digital signatures

A digital signature is a method of providing authentication using encryption, so, like a handwritten signature, it proves that the document to which it is attached does originate from the signer and that it hasn't been modified. In the context of sending an email, a digital signature is produced by a computation involving the sender's private key and the message itself. It is then attached to the message for sending. When received, other computations using the sender's public key can be carried out to verify the authenticity of the message.

Digital certificates (digital IDs)

Digital certificates are used to verify the identity of each person in an electronic transaction. Certificates are issued by trusted third-party organizations (Certificate Authorities). Certificate Authorities verify the authenticity of certificate requests, in particular the connection between a person's public key and his or her identification. They will then provide a unique digitally signed certificate which can be used as proof of identity in electronic transactions. Digital certificates may be used in a range of situations, for example as an indicator of identity for clients entering Web sites (they may replace passwords). They may map to a user's email address. Alternatively, they may download alongside a Web page to indicate that the source of the Web page is of reputable origin. Currently, certificate authority services are offered by countries and commercial bodies such as VeriSign, BelSign, Certisign Certification Digital Ltd, among others.

For special pages devoted to Public Key Infrastructure (PKI) and containing extensive lists of Certification Authorities consult: The PKI page at **http://www.pki-page.org/** and the PKI page of Commonwealth of Massachusetts at **http://www.magnet.state.ma.us/itd/legal/pki.htm**. The European Certification Authority Forum **http://www.eema.org/ecaf** provides a neutral forum for Certification Authorities, users, vendors, consultants and academic institutions to meet the demands in the marketplace for secure digital identity and trusted third-party products and services.

Status of encryption

Despite its track record as an effective security tool, obstacles to the widespread and effective use of encryption remain. A number of national governments see it not as a useful technical measure, but as potentially providing a shield for criminal or subversive activities. Governments' concerns to be able to tap into all forms of communications have led to proposals for key recovery systems (key escrow). Such systems would use a trusted third-party with which copies of private encryption keys would be deposited. Keys could then be recovered for legal purposes such as criminal investigation, if necessary.

The case of the Clipper Chip in the USA is another example of a government wishing to preserve its right of access to communications between citizens. Such measures have provoked a considerable amount of protest because they are perceived to pose a threat to privacy and security for Internet users.

Another obstacle, until very recently, was the well-known ban on the export of high grade encryption systems by the US State Department. As a result of this ban, US-developed software products such as Netscape Navigator and Microsoft

Internet Explorer used outside the USA incorporated only lower level security (40-bit) encryption. The US government have only recently agreed to drop this restriction, and companies are now beginning to take advantage of the new export rules.

One of the success stories of encryption is PGP (Pretty Good Privacy), a software package for use with email, which provides a high level of protection of privacy and is widely used. PGP is discussed in Section 5.5.

Finding more information

RSA: Frequently Asked Questions about Today's Cryptography at **http://www.rsasecurity.com/rsalabs/faq/**

Information resources on PKI and related issues at **http://www.terena.nl/projects/pki/pki-info.html**

Tools and Software for PKI-based Internet applications at **http://www.terena.nl/projects/pki/pki-swtools.html**

5.3 SECURITY ON THE WEB

With the onward rush of electronic commerce on the Internet, there is widespread concern, particularly in the commercial sector, about security on the Web. Customers want to be reassured about the safety of entrusting their credit card numbers to a Web form. Companies would like to know that they can rely on the Web as a secure medium for business transactions. Software developers have taken note of the needs, and Microsoft and Netscape have incorporated cryptography software into their respective Web browsers to facilitate secure transactions and messaging.

SSL

SSL (Secure Sockets Layer), developed by Netscape, is a protocol for secure and reliable communications between Web clients and servers. It uses encryption to keep information private in transit, authenticates the server, and ensures that data sent between client and server is not tampered with. It is implemented on both server and client. Clients which implement it include Netscape Navigator and Microsoft Internet Explorer, and it is available with servers from Apache, Netscape, Microsoft, IBM, Quarterdeck, OpenMarket and O'Reilly and Associates. SSL offers protection of commercial transactions such as giving a credit card number. It uses a secure form (the URL begins with `https://` rather than `http://`). Another indicator of SSL at work is the security icon (padlock) on the bottom of the Netscape Navigator or Internet Explorer window. If documents are not secure, the padlock is shown as open; secure documents show a closed padlock. You may also receive a pop-up window informing you that the document is secure.

SET

SET, or Secure Electronic Transaction protocol, is an open standard for the processing of credit card transactions over the Internet created jointly by Netscape, Microsoft, Visa and Mastercard. It allows different vendors' software to interoperate with other vendors' software. SET requires special software on both client and server.

IP security developments

Developments in the Internet Protocol (IP), the mechanism by which all Internet information is transported across the network, includes some security features. IPv6, the new version of IP beginning to be supported in common network software and systems, uses some of the IPSec technologies (IP Layer Security Protocol). IPSec is built into recent versions of the Solaris operating system for Unix as well as Windows 2000 from Microsoft. Incorporating security at the network level is a fundamental shift in Internet developments and will mean in the future that security is not dealt with solely at the application level.

Further information about security protocols

Security Protocols Overview: **http://www.rsasecurity.com/standards/protocols/**

IPSec (IP Layer Security Protocol): **http://csrc.nist.gov/ipsec/**

SET (Secure Electronic Transaction Protocol): **http://www.mastercard.com/shoponline/set/set.html**

5.4 SECURE EMAIL

Plain email is not a secure medium. Messages can be read by people with authorized (or unauthorized) access to mail servers which handle the mail, unlikely though this might be. There are a few basic requirements for secure and private exchange of email. To reiterate:

- Confidentiality – nobody other than the intended recipient can read the message.
- Integrity – we know that a message hasn't been tampered with in transmission.
- Authentication – we can be certain that the message comes from the person from whom it appears to come.

Where privacy, authenticity and integrity of information sent are vital, users will look for ways of making their email secure. There are a number of tools and standards available for this, though unfortunately they don't necessarily interoperate with each other. The most widely used is PGP (see Section 5.5); others include S/MIME and PEM/MOSS.

S/MIME

S/MIME, developed by RSA, is a standard for secure email which extends the MIME specification. It is a consortium effort to integrate security into MIME, backed by Microsoft, RSA and others. S/MIME was designed as a standard which would integrate into application software, giving interoperability irrespective of platform. It uses encryption to protect message privacy, digital signatures and digital certificates to authenticate senders, and a secure hashing function to detect message tampering. It boasts an easy-to-use interface in which encrypted messages are denoted by a lock, and those with digital signatures are shown with a pen icon. Products incorporating S/MIME include Netscape Messenger and Outlook Express. S/MIME cannot interoperate with MOSS or PGP. For further information on S/MIME see **http://www.rsasecurity.com/standards/smime/ resources.html**

PEM/MOSS

PEM (Privacy Enhanced Mail) is an older standard for secure email, encompassing encryption, authentication and certificate-based key management. PEM public key management is hierarchical: keys are verified at trusted Certification Authorities. MIME Object Security Services (MOSS) supersedes PEM. MOSS is not interoperable with PGP.

5.5 PGP

PGP (Pretty Good Privacy) is a widely deployed encryption and authentication program used mainly for electronic mail on the Internet. It employs a number of different encryption algorithms.

Access

Freeware PGP version is available from the International PGP Home Page at **http://www.pgpi.org/** or international sites listed there. There are versions for Windows, Mac OS, OS/2, Unix, VMS and other systems. Packaged security products incorporating PGP are available from Network Associates at **http:// www.pgp.com/**

Coverage

Features of the latest version of PGP include:

- powerful encryption including a combination of two encryption methods;
- use of digital signature to protect email from tampering and alteration;
- integration with Eudora for both the Windows and Macintosh platforms, Claris Emailer for Macintosh, and Microsoft Outlook Express – there are problems with international characters in signed messages;
- application launch from within PGP to quickly view an encrypted file;
- key server integration – automatic post of public keys to a public key server. Also searching the key server for others' public keys;
- multiplatform support – PGP supports both Windows 95/NT/2000 and Macintosh;
- choice of encryption algorithm.

PGP may be used for email and also to encrypt and store files on a personal computer.

Using

The latest version of PGP hides the complexities of the various encryption processes behind an easy-to-use interface where operations are carried out at the click of a button. What is actually happening behind the scenes when a mail message is encrypted and signed is as follows:

1 A one-way hash of the message is generated.

2 The hash value is signed with the originator's secret key using the public key algorithm.

3 The message and the signature are concatenated.

4 A random session key is created.

5 The signed message is encrypted with the session key, using a private key algorithm.

6 The session key is encrypted with the recipient's public key, using a public key algorithm.

7 The encrypted message and the encrypted session key are bundled together for sending.

Though PGP is primarily used for encrypting email, the technology is used in other products such as PGPfone **http://www.pgpi.org/products/pgpfone/** for secure Internet phone calls, and PGPdisk **http://www.pgpi.org/products/pgpdisk/** for encrypting virtual disk partitions.

5.6 SSH

SSH (Secure Shell) is a protocol which provides a secure means of logging into and executing commands on another network computer running Unix (or VMS), and transferring files between computers. It negotiates and establishes an encrypted connection between an SSH client and an SSH server, authenticating the client and server using any of several available encryption algorithms, such as RSA.

Access

Commercial products from F-Secure Corporation **http://www.europe.f-secure.com/products/ssh/**, SSH Communications Security, Ltd **http://www.ssh.com/products/ssh/**, VanDyke Technologies, Inc. **http://www.vandyke.com/**. Export restrictions may apply in some countries if IDEA or RSA encryption algorithms are used.

Information about free SSH software can be found below.

Note. SSH Communications Security considers the SSH1 protocol deprecated and does not recommend the use of it. The SSH2 protocol is in the process of becoming an IETF standard and is not subject to the security vulnerabilities found in SSH1.

Coverage

SSH is used to create secure remote login and session encryption, effectively replacing commands such as telnet, rlogin and rsh. It can be configured to give the remote user a full-featured X11 windowing environment, with secure access to mail, the Web, file sharing, ftp, and other services. SSH protects against some of the common forms of masquerade and pretence by which unauthorized persons use the Internet to gain access to other computers, for instance IP spoofing (remote hosts send out packets which pretend to come from another trusted host), forgery of names, server records, interception of passwords, etc.

Using

The SSH protocol is supported by products such as SecureCRT, a 32-bit Windows terminal emulator designed for Internet and intranet use with support for telnet and rlogin protocols. Remote sites are securely accessed by entering a hostname. Some of the options available with sessions are auto login, named sessions, ZModem file transfer, emacs mode, and SOCKS firewall support. SecureCRT is available from **http://www.vandyke.com/** though export restrictions from the USA may apply until the government's new policy is fully implemented.

Further information

SSH FAQ: **http://www.ssh.org/faq.html/**

Security software

For extensive lists of security software, see:

- Information on client and server tools at **http://www.fsecure.com/**
- Tools and Software for PKI-based Internet applications at **http://www.terena.nl/projects/pki/pki-swtools.html**
- The OpenSource page for free implementation of SSH protocol at **http://www.net.lut.ac.uk/psst/**

Free SSH clients

Open SSH Project: **http://www.openssh.com/**

List of free SSH software and other SSH resources: **http://www.freessh.org/**

LSH: Free implementation of the SSH protocol. The official GNU software: **ftp:// ftp.net.lut.ac.uk/lsh/**

Free Secure Shell Client for Windows 95/NT 4.0. Originally a UCSD Association for Computing Machinery Project: **http://pgpdist.mit.edu/FiSSH/**

Free SSH client for Windows – TTSSH: **http://www.zip.com.au/~roca/ttssh.html**

FSH: **http://www.lysator.liu.se/fsh/**. Fast remote command execution. FSH is a drop-in RSH-compatible replacement for SSH that automatically reuses SSH tunnels.

NiftyTelnet 1.1 with SSH support: **http://www.lysator.liu.se/~jonasw/freeware/ niftyssh/**. The first free SSH client for MacOS.

APPENDIX A
File formats and associated software

The following tables list some common file formats and software which will handle them (though it may not be the only software which can be used).

Table A.1 Compressed and encoded files

File extension	Definition	How to process
.exe	Self-extracting archive for PCs	No additional software needed on a PC
.gz	Gnu version of zip used on Unix	Use unzip on Unix, MacGZip on Mac, Stuffit Expander for Windows on PC Windows
.hqx	Macintosh BinHex file encoded as text	Use Xbin on Unix, Stuffit Expander on Mac, BinHex13 on PC Windows
.sit	Macintosh archiving and compression format	Use Stuffit 1.51 on Unix, Stuffit Expander on Mac, Stuffit Expander for Windows on PC Windows
.tar	Unix archive format. Tar files may also be compressed	On Unix use command: tar-xf, TAR 4.0b on Mac, WinZIP on PC Windows
.uu or .uue	File converted to text format using uuencode	To convert back to original form, use command uudecode on Unix, uuLite 3.0 on Mac, WinCode on PC. If transferred by email, mail program may handle conversion automatically
.z	Unix compressed file	To expand, use command uncompress on Unix if not done automatically by ftp program, Stuffit Expander with Expander Enhancer on Mac, WinZIP on PC Windows
.zip	pkzip PC compressed file	To expand, use Stuffit Expander w/EE on Mac, WinZIP on PC

Table A.2 Formatted document types

File extension	Definition	How to process
.doc	Common PC format for formatted text files	Microsoft Word, WordPerfect for Windows, Wordview
.pdf	Portable Document Format from Adobe, portable across computing platforms	Adobe's Acrobat Reader is needed to read pdf files
.ps	PostScript. PostScript files include formatting information primarily for printing to a PostScript printer	May be viewed with Ghostscript for Mac, Windows and Unix
.rtf	Rich Text Format. ASCII rendering of binary word-processed documents.	Programs such as Microsoft Word will convert to and from rtf files

Table A.3 Graphics and multimedia file types

File extension	Definition	How to process
.aiff	Sound format for Apple Mac. Files are downloaded then played locally	Playable with LiveAudio plug-in which comes with Netscape Navigator 3.0 and higher. Playable in Internet Explorer 3.0+. Also Sound App (Mac) from download.com (**http://download.com/**)
.asf	ASF (Advanced Streaming Format) is Microsoft's streaming format. Can include audio, video, scripts, ActiveX controls, and HTML documents	Windows Media Player (included with all Windows OS) **http:// www.microsoft.comwindows/ mediaplayer/**
.au	Sound format for Unix. Files are downloaded then played locally. Supports 8-bit sound only	Playable with LiveAudio plug-in which comes with Netscape Navigator 3.0 and higher. Internet Explorer 3.0 and higher support .au MIME type
.avi	AVI (audio/video interleaved), video file-type used by Video for Windows, Win 95's multimedia architecture	Windows Media Player. Allows easy integration of Win Word documents and PowerPoint
.dcr	Macromedia Director	Windows Media Player. Allows easy integration of Win Word documents and PowerPoint

File extension	Definition	How to process
.gif	Graphics compression format from CompuServe most suitable for line-art images	Viewable with Web browser or LView Pro (PC) **http://www.lview.com/** or Gif Converter (Mac)
.jpeg	Compression standard particularly suitable for photographic images	Viewable with graphical Web browser, also Lview Pro and PolyView
.mid, .midi	A music definition language and communications protocol rather than a format. MIDI (Musical Instrument Digital Interface) contains instructions to perform particular commands	LiveAudio plug-in for Netscape. Automatically playable with sound-enabled versions of Internet Explorer or with Media Player. Also Crescendo!, Yamaha's MIDPLUG. Midi players listed at **http://www.aitech.ac.jp/~ckelly/ help/midi-players.html**
.mov	Format for QuickTime movies	Sparkle, MoviePlayer (Mac), QuickTime for Windows (**http://www.apple.com/ quicktime/**)
.mpeg .mpg	(Motion Picture Experts Group). Widely used standard for digital compresssion of moving images. Files are played locally	MPEG viewers such as MPEGPlay, mtv-1.0, mtvp-sdk, QuickTime MPEG extension, HyperMPEG Player, XingMPEG Player (Windows), Sparkle (Mac). See a list of resources at MPEG.ORG at **http:// www.mpeg.org/MPEG/MPEG-content.html** for extensive list of pointers
.MP3	MPEG Audio Layer 3. Advanced compression technique for small near-CD-quality audio files	Windows Media Player, Sonique (**http://www.sonique.com/**)
.png	PNG (Portable Network Graphics) is an extensible file format for faster images intended as a patent-free replacement for the GIF format	Supported by Internet Explorer 4.0+
.qt	QuickTime movie file type from Apple – files are played locally	Playable with QuickTime players such as QuickTime for Windows (**http:// www.apple.com/quicktime/**). Player is included in Netscape Navigator 3.0+ and Internet Explorer 4.0+

File extension	Definition	How to process
.qt3	QuickTime 3. Advanced compression format for video, audio, MIDI, animation, 3-D, etc.	Playable with QuickTime players
.ra, .rm, .ram	Real Audio, pioneering format for streaming audio on the Web optimized for low-to-medium speed connections	RealPlayer (**http://www.real.com/**), Windows Media Player
.rv	Real Video, format for streaming video on the Web optimized for low-to-medium speed connections	RealPlayer (**http://www.real.com/**), Windows Media Player
.swf	Shockwave Flash from Macromedia for delivery of graphics and animation on the Internet	Shockwave, Flash player
.tiff	High-resolution image format	JPEGView (Mac) Lview Pro (PC)
.viv	VIVO format for compression of streaming video, particularly over low bandwidth	**http://www.vivo.com/**
.vrml	VRML (Virtual Reality Modeling Language) is an open standard for the definition of 3-D environments used on the Web	Simple VRML files can be created with a plain-text editor, or for more complex model building, modeling software will probably be required. VRML files are viewed with a VRML helper application or browser plug-in such as WorldView
.wav	Windows sound format	Playable with LiveAudio plug-in which comes with Netscape Navigator 3.0 and higher. Playable in Internet Explorer 3.0. Also with Windows Media Player (included with all latest Windows installations)

References

Compression FAQ: **http://www.faqs.org/faqs/compression-faq/part1/ section-2.html**

BrowserWatch Plug-In Plaza **http://browserwatch.internet.com/plug-in.html** for extensive lists of multimedia, graphics, sound, and other plug-ins, browsable by category, or by platform.

http://download.com/ for playing and viewing programs.

Netscape's list of Browser plug-ins **http://home.netscape.com/plugins/index.html**

GLOSSARY

ActiveX ActiveX is a technology developed by Microsoft. With an ActiveX-enabled browser (i.e. Internet Explorer only) ActiveX controls can be downloaded as part of a Web document to add functionality to the browser (similar to Java applets). In particular, ActiveX enables seamless viewing of Windows files of all types, e.g. spreadsheets, and in combination with other technologies such as Java and scripting languages, makes possible the development of complex Web applications. Currently it runs on 32-bit Windows platforms (Windows 95 and NT) only.

Avatar A graphical image of a user, such as used in graphical real-time chat applications, or, a graphical personification of a computer or a computer process, intended to make the computing or network environment a more friendly place.

Caching Web documents retrieved may be stored (cached) for a time so that they can be conveniently accessed if further requests are made for them. The issue of whether the most up-to-date copy of the file is retrieved is handled by the caching program which initially makes a brief check and compares the date of the file at its original location with that of the copy in the cache. If the date of the cached file is the same as the original, then the cached copy is used.

Web browsers normally maintain a cache of retrieved documents and this cache is used for retrievals where possible. In addition, the user may configure the browser to point to a caching server via the browser's options or preferences. File requests not able to be supplied from the browser cache would then be directed to the caching server. The caching server would supply the files from its cache if they were current, or pass on the request to the originating server if they were not.

Client–server Client–server refers to a model of interaction between computers which is commonly used on the Internet. Users employ client software, such as a Web browser, to request information from servers. Servers, such as WWW servers, supply information in response to requests from clients. The client, which is normally installed on the user's computer, displays the information for the user. For instance when a Web document is retrieved from a remote server, the client will interpret the **HTML** tags and display the document appropriately. Some aspects of how documents are delivered and displayed may be determined by the user through configuration of the client's settings, for instance size and color of font, whether images are displayed, whether **cookies** are accepted.

In the client–server model, clients and servers have a special relationship derived from the common use of a well-defined set of communicating conventions (protocol). For example, Web browsers and servers use the WWW protocol, **HTTP**. Web browsers generally can use other Internet protocols as well. In this way they can also retrieve information from ftp servers, gopher servers, etc.

The client–server model of processing is one of the cornerstones of the Internet's success. It is an efficient system which distributes the processing load between client and server, and also gives the user some control over their own interface to Internet information.

Cookies Cookies provide a means for a Web server to induce a client to store information about itself which can subsequently be called up by the Web server when required. This might be information which users have supplied about themselves, their preferences or their requirements via forms input. The oft-cited example is the shopping list which might be added to from time to time. Cookies are currently implemented by Netscape and Internet Explorer.

More information: **http://www.netscape.com/newsref/std/cookie_spec.html**

HTML WWW documents are normally written in HyperText Markup Language (HTML), the native language of the Web. HTML enables links to be specified, and also the structure and formatting of Web documents to be defined. HTML documents are written in plain text, with the addition of tags that describe or define the text they enclose. For example, a link is defined by the ANCHOR <A> tag placed around the hyperlinked text. It specifies the URL of the 'linked to' document, e.g.

```
<A HREF="http://www.terena.nl/gnrt/websearch/index.html"Web
Search Tools</A
```

HTML is an evolving standard. Current work is focused on extending accessibility features, multimedia objects, scripting, style sheets, layout, forms, mathematics and internationalization. See the World Wide Web Consortium site **http://www.w3.org/** for current information.

HTTP HTTP (HyperText Transfer Protocol) is the foundation protocol of the World Wide Web. It sets the rules for exchanges between browser and server. It provides for the transfer of hypertext and hypermedia, for recognition of file types, and other functions.

Hyperlink Example of hyperlink in an HTML document:

```
<A HREF="http://www.terena.nl/gnrt/websearch/index.html"Web
Search Tools</A
```

When the HTML document is viewed with the Web browser, the tag information between angle brackets is not visible, but the words *Web Search Tools* are displayed in whatever format or color is defined for links by the browser or the document's author (the browser default is often blue, underlined text but HTML authors may specify any color or style). When the user selects these words, the document *index.html* will be displayed, having been fetched from the Web server *www.terena.nl*, where it was found in the path */gnrt/websearch*.

Imagemap Imagemaps, also known as *active maps* are graphics containing active link areas. Instead of the link being from a word or phrase in the document, it is embedded in a defined area of the imagemap. Clicking on that area fetches the referenced document. Imagemaps are often used to provide a graphical entry point to a Web site, though a text-based route through the site should always be given as an alternative.

ISDN ISDN (Integrated Services Digital Network) is a system of digital telephone connections. It allows multiple digital channels to be operated simultaneously through a single, standard interface. The Basic Rate Interface (BRI) consists of two 64 kbps plus another lower rate channel to handle signaling. Primary Rate Interface (PRI) consists of 23 channels plus a signaling channel. ISDN is adequate for videoconferencing and other high bandwidth applications. The cost of an ISDN line is higher than a normal phone line, and special equipment is required.

JAVA Powerful, cross-platform programming language developed by Sun Microsystems. Java applets (small applications) may be incorporated into Web documents and can be executed securely by any Java-capable browser irrespective of whether it is running on a PC, an Apple Mac or a Unix workstation. Both Netscape Navigator and Internet Explorer are Java-capable. Java is being used in many ways which enhance the functionality and interactivity of Web pages.

JavaScript   Scripting language (originally called LiveScript) developed by Netscape Communications for use with the Navigator browser. JavaScript code forms part of the HTML page and can be used for example to respond to user actions such as button clicks or to run processes locally or validate data. JScript is the Microsoft equivalent of Netscape's JavaScript for use with Microsoft's Internet Explorer.

MIME   The World Wide Web's ability to recognize and handle files of different types is largely dependent on the use of the MIME (Multipurpose Internet Mail Extensions) standard. The standard provides for a system of registration of file types with information about the applications needed to process them. This information is incorporated into Web server and browser software, and enables the automatic recognition and display of registered file types.

Users can add other file types and associated processing instructions to their browser's configuration options if they wish.

Multicast   A multicast message is one that is transmitted to selected multiple recipients who have joined the appropriate multicast group. The sender has to generate only a single data stream. A multicast-enabled router will forward a multicast to a particular network only if there are multicast receivers on that network. Other stations filter out multicast packets at the hardware level (e.g. Ethernet or Token Ring).

PHP   PHP is a server-side, cross-platform, **HTML**-embedded scripting language that lets you create dynamic Web pages. PHP-enabled Web pages are treated just like regular HTML pages and you can create and edit them in the same way you normally create regular HTML pages.

Plug-ins   Browsers can display certain file types such as **HTML** and GIF as a standard part of their functioning. The display of other file types may be handled by additional software, either designed to work in conjunction with the browser for the display of a specific file type (a plug-in) or a stand-alone application which the browser can launch for viewing a file requiring that application (a helper application). With plug-ins there is closer integration with the functioning of the browser. Plug-ins are loaded when the browser is launched so can act instantly and non-intrusively when called upon, thus giving the browser the appearance of enhanced functionality. The idea of plug-ins was developed by Netscape but is also supported by Internet Explorer. Some plug-ins may be bundled with browser software, but many more from third-party developers are available for downloading.

Examples: Macromedia Shockwave is used to display multimedia files from Macromedia Director; Adobe Acrobat Reader is used to display PDF files.

Further information on Netscape's plug-ins **http://home.netscape.com/ plugins/index.html**

PNG Portable Network Graphics (PNG) format was designed to be a patent-free successor to the GIF format. Though not designed specifically for the Web, PNG offers particular benefits in this environment such as improved image compression (10 to 30 percent smaller than GIFs), two-dimensional interlacing, storage of text with an image making it possible for search engines to gather information and offer subject searching for images in a standard way.

Proxy server Where a high level of security is required, a proxy Web server may be used to provide a gateway between a local area network and the Internet. The local network is protected by firewall software installed on the proxy server. This software enables the proxy server to keep the two worlds separate. All outward **HTTP** requests from the local network pass through the proxy server, and similarly all information retrieved comes back in via the proxy server and is then passed back to the client. Using the options or preferences, Web browsers can be configured to point to the proxy server. Proxy servers will normally maintain a **cache** of retrieved documents.

SMIL With the World Wide Web Consortium's Synchronized Multimedia Integration Language (SMIL) standard, a language for building time-based, streaming multimedia presentations that combine audio, video, images and text is defined. Like **HTML**, SMIL is a markup language, but unlike HTML, it offers controls such as sequence, timing and multiple runtime options which are selected by the user's browser, and a means of assembling separate media objects into a single coherent presentation. It has been described as 'a universal glue for joining all kinds of different formats and types of media in interesting and useful ways'. An early implementation of SMIL is RealNetworks' G2 RealPlayer.

Last specification SMIL 2.0: **http://www.w3.org/TR/smil20/**

SVG Scalable Vector Graphics is an emerging Web standard for two-dimensional graphics. Like **HTML**, SVG is written in plain text and rendered by the browser, except that in this case, it is not just text that is rendered but also shapes and images, which can be animated and made interactive. SVG is written in **XML** and developed by the World Wide Web Consortium.

URL The Uniform Resource Locator (URL) provides a way of uniquely specifying the address of any document on the Internet. This is the lynchpin of the WWW's embedded linking. The typical URL specifies the method used to access the resource (the protocol), the name of the host computer on which it is located, and the path of the resource, e.g.

http://www.terena.nl/gnrt/websearch/index.html

The protocol specified in this example is **HTTP**, the protocol of the World Wide Web. Other protocols can also be used within the WWW.

VRML Virtual Reality Modeling Language (VRML) is an Internet standard for the rendering of 3-D graphics. VRML files can be viewed with plug-ins such as Live3D.

XML XML (Extensible Markup Language) is a standard for creating markup languages which describe the structure of data. It is not a fixed set of elements like **HTML**, but rather, it is like SGML (Standard Generalized Markup Language) in that it is a meta-language, or a language for describing languages. XML enables authors to define their own tags. XML is a formal specification of the World Wide Web Consortium. To find XML editors, see 'Whirlwind Guide to SGML tools' **http://www.infotek.no/sgmltool/editetc.htm** and also **http://www.stud.ifi.uio.no/~larsga/linker/XMLtools.html**

XSL XSL (Extensible Style Language) is a style sheet language aimed at activities such as rearranging the document that are not supported by Cascading Style Sheets (CSS), though XSL and CSS share the same underlying concepts. XSL can be used to style **XML** documents using sets of rules and definitions of actions to be applied. XSL is a specification from the World Wide Web Consortium.

WYSIWYG What You See Is What You Get. A graphical interface to a process which shows how the end-result will look as it is being produced, e.g. a WYSIWYG **HTML** editor generates HTML markup but displays the document as if viewed with a Web browser.

Further information

Free On-Line Dictionary of Computing: FOLDOC defines and explains over 12,000 Internet and computing terms in a very user-friendly format. It is produced by Imperial College, London and is authoritative, accurate and up to date.

BIBLIOGRAPHY

File formats

Allison Zhang: *Multimedia file formats on the Internet*
http://www.lib.rochester.edu/multimed/contents.htm

Compression FAQ (in 3 parts)
http://www.cs.ruu.nl/wais/html/na-dir/compression-faq/.html
Information on formats and tools for all platforms.

LEARN THE NET: File formats and extensions
http://www.learnthenet.com/english/html/34filext.htm

Mailing lists

LISTSERV – The Mailing List Management Classic
http://www.lsoft.com/listserv.stm

Netiquette

Arlene Rinaldi: *The Net: User guidelines and etiquette*
http://www.fau.edu/netiquette/net/

Dear Emily Postnews
http://www.clari.net/brad/emily.html

Security

W3C Security Resources
http://www.w3.org/Security/

Cryptography: The study of encryption (list of links)
http://world.std.com/~franl/crypto/

Web authoring

International WebMasters Association
http://www.iwanet.org/

HTML Writers Guild
http://www.hwg.org/

Joe Burns: *HTML Goodies: The tutorials*
http://www.htmlgoodies.com/tutors/

Compendium of HTML Elements
http://www.htmlcompendium.org/

Barebones Guide to HTML
http://werbach.com/barebones/barebone.html

Sizzling Jalfrezi HTML
http://www.jalfrezi.com/iniframe.htm

Web Developer's Virtual Library
http://www.stars.com/

Web Master's Reference Library
http://webreference.com/

Lynch & Horton: *Yale C/AIM Web Style Guide*
http://info.med.yale.edu/caim/manual/contents.html
Still containing a lot of useful information.

Web browsers

CNET's Browsers Topic Centre
http://www.browsers.com/

BrowserWatch
http://browserwatch.internet.com/

ZDNet's Internet Browsers
http://www.zdnet.com/zdhelp/filters/internet/browsers/

Web graphics and multimedia

Beginner's Guide to MIDI
http://www.chadales.demon.co.uk/pages/midi1.html

Royal Frazier: *All About GIF89a*
http://member.aol.com/royalef/gifabout.htm

JPEG FAQ
http://www.faqs.org/faqs/jpeg-faq/

Multimedia Authoring Web
http://www.mcli.dist.maricopa.edu/authoring/
Extensive searchable and classified collection of resources and tools.

MP3.com
http://www.mp3.com/

comp.lang.vrml FAQ
http://hiwaay.net/~crispen/vrml/faq.html
Answers basic questions and also points to current VRML standards.

Search Engine Tips from Submit It!
http://www.submit-it.com/subopt.htm

Web searching

Search Engine Watch
http://www.searchenginewatch.com/

WebTools Company: *Tutorial: Guide to effective searching on the Internet*
http://www.thewebtools.com/tutorial/tutorial.htm

University of California Berkeley Library: *Finding Information on the Internet*: A tutorial
http://www.lib.berkeley.edu/TeachingLib/Guides/Internet/FindInfo.html

Angela Elkordy: *Web Searching, Sleuthing and Sifting*
http://www.thelearningsite.net/cyberlibrarian/ismain.html

INDEX